PRINCIPAL TRAINING ON THE GROUND

ENSURING HIGHLY QUALIFIED LEADERSHIP

Sandra J. Stein and Liz Gewirtzman

Foreword by Anthony J. Alvarado
Afterword by Elaine Fink

HEINEMANN
Portsmouth, NH

Heinemann
A division of Reed Elsevier Inc.
361 Hanover Street
Portsmouth, NH 03801–3912
www.heinemann.com

Offices and agents throughout the world

Library of Congress Cataloging-in-Publication Data
Stein, Sandra J.
  Principal training on the ground : ensuring highly qualified
leadership / Sandra J. Stein and Liz Gewirtzman ; foreword and afterword
by Anthony J. Alvarado and Elaine Fink.
    p. cm.
  ISBN 0-325-00465-X (alk. paper)
  1. School principals—Training of—New York (State)—New York—Case
studies. 2. School management and organization—New York (State)—New
York—Case studies. 3. Educational leadership—New York (State)—New
York—Case studies. 4. Education, Urban—New York (State)—New
York—Case studies. I. Gewirtzman, Liz. II. Title.

LB2831.924.N7S94 2003
371.2'012'071—dc21   2003011649

Editor: Lois Bridges
Production service: Melissa L. Inglis
Production coordination: Vicki Kasabian
Cover design: Catherine Hawkes, Cat and Mouse
Typesetter: Argosy Publishing
Manufacturing: Steve Bernier

Printed in the United States of America on acid-free paper
07 06 05 04 03 VP 1 2 3 4 5

CONTENTS

Contents

FOREWORD

When we first sat down with Sandra Stein and her colleagues from the School of Public Affairs at Baruch College of the City, University of New York, to discuss what would become the Aspiring Leaders Program (ALPS), our purpose was to solve an immediate problem for District 2. We needed strong principals to lead our schools, and the existing system wasn't generating enough superior candidates to fill the jobs. We wondered if it would be possible to create a program that would give promising educators the right mix of practical and academic training. Would it make sense to create that program in collaboration with the School of Public Affairs at Baruch? As readers of this insightful account will learn, the answer to both questions was "yes."

ALPS quickly met the short-term objective of the district by producing a corps of well-trained candidates. Over the next few years, the program was refined and expanded to serve additional New York City districts, and its outlines have since been applied in San Diego and other cities, as well. Yet, that simple success story understates the real significance of the program. For reasons that are clearer today than they were in the mid-1990s, ALPS offers important lessons about how we can address such core issues as school leadership, accountability, collaboration, and culture within the context of school reform.

The assumption that the quality of the principal is directly linked to the quality of instruction and student learning has been embedded in nearly every major school reform strategy of the past two decades. But if high quality school leaders are so important, it must be determined where they come from and whose responsibility it is to develop them. These questions have attracted relatively little attention or investment, especially in urban school systems.

The ALPS program advanced the theory that the development of school leaders is a core responsibility of the school system itself. This is a radical departure from the conventional view, which holds that school leaders are out there somewhere, and that all a school system can do is advertise and try to draw them in.

In District 2, "growing" our own school leaders meant taking on the work of developing and supporting our side of ALPS, but it also meant changing the way we responded to educators within our own organization—to principals and teachers who would become the next generation of principals. Recognizing and encouraging leadership potential became far more important to us, as did supporting new principals once they were appointed.

In addition, taking responsibility for the development of school leaders also meant shifting a district's attitude toward school accountability. For example, the accountability mechanisms built into the *No Child Left Behind Act of 2001* assume that school systems will remove ineffective principals. The reality is that superintendents are unlikely to remove principals unless they have qualified people to take their places. The best baseball teams are the ones that concentrate on building their farm teams. School systems that do the same—that is, those that invest time and money in the development of up-and-coming school leaders—will be at a distinct advantage when faced with the need to replace a weak principal with a strong one.

Our work with Baruch also shed light on another facet of school reform—the training provided by schools of education is insufficient and irrelevant to the real challenges of running a school or a classroom. What ALPS revealed was that both school systems and universities need to think and act differently if they want to change that situation. To develop and run its side of the collaboration, the district needs to give far more time, money, and attention to training principals than it has done in the past. Meanwhile, our collaborators at Baruch acknowledged that the school district, not the individual student, is their ultimate customer, and that the relevant measure of success is the ability of program graduates to lead school improvement. In response to this, Baruch professors worked with practitioners to craft courses that blended theory and practice in unconventional ways.

The collaboration proved that real dialogue is not only possible but necessary. Baruch had a strong intellectual and institutional commitment to rethinking its role, but the university would not have been able to carry out that task effectively without the full, ongoing engagement of the school system. For the moment, schools of education have a monopoly on state certification that has insulated them from the need to change. However, as school systems are pressed to improve by state and federal accountability systems, schools of education will need to get much better at discerning and responding to the needs of schools. The alternative will be to risk losing their franchise to experimentation and deregulation.

Finally, as the story told by Liz and Sandra makes clear, ALPS exemplifies the kind of work districts need to take on if they are serious about the reform agenda. Some of the strongest sections of the book give detailed accounts of how key people from District 2 and Baruch thought through and solved problems in entrepreneurial and innovative ways; how they looked for evidence of what was working and what wasn't; how they extracted theory and broke it down for real-world application; how they blended intellectual and practical knowledge about how adults and children learn and how good schools are run. There are general lessons here about how school systems and schools of education must learn to behave.

We came late to this work in New York, establishing ALPS in District 2 only in my eighth year as superintendent. We got to it much earlier in San Diego—in the third year of a citywide campaign of school reform. Recently, I have urged superintendents to start training school leaders immediately—in the first year or so of a new administration—especially if accountability measures are being phased in. My own experience suggests that this book will be abundantly useful to educators around the country, as they rise to the challenge of preparing the practical, intellectual, and problem-solving leaders our schools so urgently need.

ANTHONY J. ALVARADO
CHANCELLOR OF INSTRUCTION,
INSTITUTE FOR LEARNING, SAN DIEGO CITY SCHOOLS;
FORMER CHANCELLOR, NEW YORK CITY BOARD OF EDUCATION;
FORMER SUPERINTENDENT,
NEW YORK CITY COMMUNITY SCHOOL
DISTRICTS FOUR AND TWO

ACKNOWLEDGMENTS

The program described here represents the work of many people.

To the folks whose vision and persistence allowed this program to take root, Anthony J. Alvarado, Elaine Fink, Carroll Seron, Lois Cronholm, and Matthew Goldstein, we thank you for taking a risk in developing the partnership.

To the folks whose brilliance, tenacity, and commitment nurtured and cultivated the partnership: from the districts—Shelley Harwayne, Tanya Kaufman (a.k.a. "the Mother of ALPS"), Fay Pallen, Carmen Fariña, Laura Koch, Jorge Izquierdo, Roser Salavert, Pat Romandetto, Barbara Goldman, Lesley Gordon, Robert Riccobono, Lucille Swarns, and Richard Organiscak; and from Baruch College School of Public Affairs—Stan Altman, David Birdsell, and Lynne Weikart—we thank you for always focusing on making the relationship stronger.

To the folks who contributed generously and thoughtfully to the program's existence and growth—Larry Becker, David Bloomfield, Gloria Buckery, Anna Marie Carrillo, Regina Chiou, Chris Daley, Allison Douglas-Chicoye, Katherine Ilovar-Rodriguez, Chris Mazzeo, Jill Myers, Rhonda Perry, Daria Rigney, Michael Schlar, Lisa Siegman, Anna Switzer, Myrna Wapner, Lily Woo, Ron Woo, and Leslie Zackman—we thank you for your hard work and support.

And to all of the aspiring leaders, now principals, assistant principals, staff developers, and educational leaders, we thank you for making the program better for the next cohort, every single time.

We thank the Stupski Foundation, which generously supported our documentation of the Aspiring Leaders Program, as well as a conference on principal preparation that was critical to our thinking and shaped the foundation of this book.

We thank Lois Bridges for her commitment to sharing the work of the Aspiring Leaders Program with concerned educators nationwide. And, we are forever indebted to Petra Rappoccio for her diligent research and careful organization.

Liz and Sandra thank Matt Lambiase for his editorial com-mitment and for keeping us both sane in the process.

In addition, Liz thanks Andrew Lachman, Dóri Gewirtzman, and Lev Gewirtzman for their encouragement, and all the relationships, both failed and enduring, that made her the woman she is today.

Sandra thanks Matt, Chloe, and Liz.

INTRODUCTION

Shortly after Constancia Warren, senior program officer for the education division and director of the Urban High School Initiative for the Carnegie Corporation of New York, observed Sandra teach a class in the School of Public Affairs' principal preparation program, she called Liz to report that for the first time she believed that it was possible to learn to be a principal. For us, this was a very significant statement.

Central to our work as instructors charged with preparing principals to meet the challenges of urban schools is the idea that while the knowledge and skills that make an instructional leader successful are complex, they are not essentially mysterious. That is, if subjected to careful and persistent inquiry, they can be named, described, and taught to aspiring leaders, using a "learning through doing" approach to adult learning.

To develop a principal preparation program powerful enough to reliably generate principals capable of improving instruction for every student in every classroom in an urban school, we mined the knowledge held by expert practitioners, the experiences of novice principals, research-based theories of teaching and learning, and organizational development theory. The instructional leadership characteristics that emerged from this process, and that we have since learned to teach to aspiring leaders, include:

- having a strong vision and values that orient all school activities toward student learning and academic growth, so as to build a culture of instruction

- creating a sense of urgency and excitement about teaching and learning, so as to maximize the effectiveness of any curricular approach through learning about instruction
- organizing the resources of time (through school programming), and money (through school budgeting), and people (through strategic management practices) to support the instructional agenda
- knowing how to recognize the assets in a school community and how to build on those assets for the purpose of student learning
- positioning one's self as the lead teacher and lead learner in the school, and seeing one's self in the role of facilitator of adult learning in the service of student learning
- continuously working to improve one's own practice while applying consistent pressure and support to improve the teaching staff
- analyzing student performance data and using it to determine what teachers need to learn, where to start implementing a new approach, and how to measure whether the implementation is effective
- thinking strategically about schools as systems to leverage change, anticipating resistance and staying focused on continual instructional improvement
- sharing leadership and building leadership capacity among one's professional staff, so that practitioners continually experiment together to improve their practice
- modeling the behaviors one wishes to see in the school community
- valuing parent and community participation in the instructional agenda, and making the language of schooling accessible to support that participation
- "managing up" and advocating for the school with supervisors by involving them in thinking through tough instructional challenges

The program faculty, in this case, were administrators and practitioners from New York City school districts and university professors from the School of Public Affairs at Baruch College of the City University of New York. This book is intended to make available for further learning both the process we engaged in and the teaching and learning materials we developed. It represents our collective understanding (at a particular point in time) in a constantly evolving process of co-construction, practice, reflection, and improvement.

Although the work took place in a specific location, we believe that the knowledge gleaned may be useful to a diverse audience of school district administrators, university administrators, professors, and practitioners, as well as local, state, and federal policy makers.

The conditions under which this innovative program was developed were unique to our circumstances. While acknowledging this "uniqueness," we would like to raise here the issue of how school districts might go about generating favorable conditions for productive collaborative work with universities.

In thinking about this question, we see a continuum of options. On the one hand, school districts could become more aggressive in their demand that principal preparation programs produce the quality of leadership they need to improve instruction in their schools by taking advantage of their position as primary employers. In states where school district/university partnerships are encouraged or required for accreditation of principal preparation programs, school districts that are able to articulate and assess the leadership knowledge and skills they need could positively influence the rules of engagement for those partnerships. In states that do not explicitly promote school district/university partnerships for developing school leaders, principal selection processes and criteria that include demonstrated acquisition of the desired knowledge and skill could over time have a positive influence on university-run principal preparation programs by increasing communication between those preparing instructional leaders and those employing them. On the other hand, in states that are awarding school districts the ability to provide alternative routes to principal certification, school districts could design and run their own preparation programs, positively influencing university-run programs through a competitive market strategy.

Whatever the strategy employed, we believe that the time has come to marshal our collective intellectual capital and focus our attention on creating the conditions necessary to provide each and every school with the instructional leadership it needs.

CHAPTER ONE

THE PRACTICE IN THEORY

Many scholars and practitioners have asked the core designers and instructors of the Aspiring Leaders Program questions similar to those asked of married couples by their single friends: "How do you do it?" "How do you resolve fights?" "How do you make decisions?" "How do you know whether the relationship works?"

The process of developing a principal preparation program—which brought together school districts and a university—did resemble the unfolding of a romantic relationship. As with most enduring relationships, we have had our moments of certainty, followed by moments of doubt and ambivalence.

Our motivation for agreeing to the endeavor was by no means altruistic. As educators, we needed viable responses to changes in the environment in which we worked. These pressures, similar to those felt nationwide, included: increasing demands on superintendents to bring students to high standards of performance at accelerated rates; the exodus of veteran principals from school districts due to retirement; the paucity of skilled, well-prepared candidates available to fill the positions left vacant by retirees; the expectation that universities should align preparatory programs with emerging national and state standards for principal leadership; and the need for states to "do something" about the school leadership pipeline.

The Aspiring Leaders Program, a partnership between Baruch College's School of Public Affairs and New York City's Community School District Two, was created to manage these pressures. We hope that others can benefit from the lessons we learned as our relationship formed and grew.

What we offer here is not a blueprint. It is instead the story of how we went about the work of organizing the knowledge and learning experiences we came to believe to be essential to principal leadership development in a way that fostered accountability. It was shaped by the context—especially the attributes and characteristics of those who co-constructed it—and it represents a point in time in an evolving process of co-constructed, continuous improvement. It comes with a label, warning us of the dangers of adopting the products of other people's reform efforts.

In his book *Change Forces: The Sequel*, Michael Fullan (1999) points out that often the results of reform efforts "fail to be replicated because the wrong thing is being replicated—the reform itself, instead of the conditions which spawned its success" (64). Similarly, Healey and De Stefano (1997) explain the following:

> People's educational aspirations, needs and contexts differ from place to place. Accordingly, what works in one location won't necessarily work in another. And even in those instances where an "outside" innovation addresses some of the specific needs and aspirations of a particular location, its fate is still precarious, for unless there is widespread ownership of the innovation (a factor largely engendered through the development of local solutions), chances are that it will not become a permanent part of that location's educational landscape. Instead of replication of the reform itself, we contend that it is the *conditions which give rise to the reform in the first place* that should be replicated. (10–11)

We hope that the reader will take this warning to heart and make use of our story and the examples the text provides in the spirit in which they are offered—as insight into an accountable, co-constructive process. But first, we need to establish a common understanding of the problems we aimed to address when we decided to come together, problems that are undoubtedly not unique.

THE PROBLEM

Since state education departments typically require college credits toward administrative certification, university systems are responsible for credentialing school-based practitioners. States accredit university programs based on written documents about the scope of the required courses they offer, and other supplementary information about the program faculty and overall design. Based on this arrangement, colleges engaged in practitioner preparation are able to attract a reliable influx of students. Traditionally, university faculty members are autonomous actors with primary authority over their course content, pedagogical approach, assignments, and grading systems. For example, course outlines rarely require review or approval by any governing body. In fact, sections of the same course taught by different professors may have entirely different substantive contents, pedagogical approaches, required assignments, and assessment strategies. University professors are encouraged to teach their areas of expertise, focusing courses on their particular research agendas and preferred bodies of literature. Programs, therefore, are not necessarily cohesive, coherent, or consistent between different groups of faculty members in the same college.

The school leadership knowledge base at the university is grounded in the review or generation of scholarly research. At the university, the generation of new knowledge happens most commonly through systematic analysis of the empirical world. It is grounded in observations of schooling practice; interviews and surveys of school-based practitioners, parents, and students, or numerical data sets based on variables such as student performance; or through reflective and theoretical engagement in educational issues relevant to school leadership. Research projects are typically designed by scholars who first generate a researchable question, then seek access to a site or various sites of practice, collect relevant data, analyze those data, and write scholarly reports for an academic audience. The time that it takes to produce quality work is substantial. In fact, the amount of time that elapses between peer review, the process that determines which articles will be published in scholarly journals, and the actual date of publication may be as long as eighteen to twenty-four months (Natriello 1999). At best, the process of generating new knowledge is rigorous, systematic, and slow. By the time a research finding is published, the empirical world of practice has moved on, confronting new challenges and new realities. University faculty members harbor a great deal of knowledge about various elements of schooling, but the actual practice of leading a school for instruction is often beyond the knowledge and experiential domain of most professors. Most professors do not actually participate in the construction of that knowledge.

University incentive structures do not encourage or require participation in school leadership practice on the part of professors. Faculty members are typically hired based on their record or promise of scholarly publication, not on their knowledge and experience of, or commitment to, effective school-based leadership practices. The professional competence and worth of faculty members are determined primarily by their number of publications, and only secondarily (if at all) on their ability to facilitate the development of useful skills and knowledge for future practitioners. While a faculty member's published research is reviewed by colleagues and used in both external and internal reviews for tenure and promotion, her or his teaching is rarely, if at all, observed by colleagues. As a consequence, professional development for the teaching aspects of a professor's work are underemphasized in many universities. The construction of new practice-based knowledge for the purposes of preparing practitioners is secondary to the reporting of such knowledge for scholarly and policy-oriented consumption.

There are then no formal accountability mechanisms to ensure that university program graduates learn anything useful for their future practice. Aspiring leaders pay their tuition, take the required courses, receive state certification, and move into school leadership positions. Whether or not they are able to lead instruction and improve student learning is not considered a reflection of the effectiveness of their preparatory program.

Given the above, it should come as no surprise that scholars and practitioners alike have identified a gulf between administrative training programs and the tools, skills, and knowledge necessary for successful practice (see Daresh 1997; Elmore 2001; Glasman and

Glasman 1997; Griffiths 1988; Kempner 1991; Orozco 2001; Thurston, Clift, and Schacht 1993). Coupled with a dearth of qualified new candidates available to assume leadership positions as current principals retire or leave the profession (Hertling 1999; Keller 1998; Wilmore and McNeil 1999), we now face what many have called a "crisis in school leadership" (see, for example, American Association of Colleges for Teacher Education 2001; Orozco 2001; Steinberg 2000; Tucker and Codding 2002). In some areas, there is not in fact a shortage of licensed candidates, but rather a shortage of qualified candidates (see Orozco 2001). As Richard Elmore (2001) has argued, "We're faced with a system . . . a huge reserve pool of people who are credentialed . . . and we don't have a clue about whether they can actually run a performance-based organization" (32). This crisis is most acute for district-level administrators who are hoping to fill vacancies with strong instructional leaders.

At their worst, traditional educational administration programs are part of what Elmore (2001) has referred to as a "three-way cartel" between state departments of education, universities, and school districts. Within this cartel a fascinating round of the so-called blame game sometimes emerges. Districts blame universities for offering irrelevant and outdated courses. Universities blame districts for impeding the implementation of certain reforms, for adapting unfashionable instructional approaches, and for sending ill-prepared practitioners to receive certification. Both districts and universities blame the state for maintaining models of certification that seem more responsive to bureaucratic procedures and political interests than to building powerful programs. At a time when most educational institutions are faced with performance-based accountability structures for the quality of their work, university programs have not been held accountable for the quality of their programs on any coherent or consistent basis. All parties recognize that it is time for a change.

ATTEMPTED SOLUTIONS

Those who have tried to resolve these tensions have commonly used four approaches. The first is to persuade the state education department to allow school districts to develop their own professional workforce, thereby deregulating the market monopoly of the universities. This tactic has taken hold rather recently in some states, including Louisiana, Florida, and Massachusetts, with other states soon to follow. Or, when the state does not alter its regulations, districts rely on university program improvement or some cash-for-credit arrangement in which the university plays a nominal role in exchange for tuition dollars. The three other approaches involve some combination of professors and practitioners situated within traditional university structures.

The second approach is to hire practitioners to teach principal preparation courses as adjunct instructors. Universities generally provide minimal guidance or direction for the courses to be taught. What these practitioners choose to do as adjunct instructors may or may not have any connection to the overall program of study; may or may not duplicate the readings or assignments required in other courses; and may or may not reflect, build on, or nurture the information that students encounter in other courses.

A third approach is to make the "parallel play" of the two systems more proximal. Here, practitioners and professors each contribute what they think aspiring leaders should know and be able to do, and together they give that information to students without any formal attempt to synthesize their views. Typically, professors provide the theoretical perspective, while practitioners discuss the daily realities, but the knowledge they communicate is rarely integrated. To adapt the metaphor of the "Christmas Tree Schools," decorated with the ornaments of various reform efforts that never come together as a collective whole (Bryk, Easton, Kerbow, Rollow, and Sebring 1993), these programs produce "Christmas Tree Leaders," practitioners who understand isolated facts, theories, and practices, but have not yet learned how to use them in a fluid effort toward meaningful school improvement.

A final approach is to make compromises in the knowledge amassed from both domains. In this model, the vast, fragmented body of knowledge that includes both scholarship and practice is watered down for transmission. Through a process of negotiation, professors and practitioners decide what material they will include and what they will leave out, but make no attempt to integrate their knowledge domains or to construct new knowledge about principal preparation.

The last two approaches can be carried out through a co-teaching model of course delivery. In the co-teaching model, professors and practitioners come together in one classroom and impart what they know from their respective situations. Instead of engaging in a deep exploration of the knowledge future leaders should develop and master in preservice programs, the co-teachers present what they know, side by side. In the more organized examples of this practice, co-instructors divide up the time during course meetings; arrange who will speak when; and share the responsibility of teaching. However, these models tend not to stray from traditional university approaches in any meaningful way; they just bring practitioners in to carry out some of the traditional work. We therefore propose the creation of something new.

OUR SOLUTION

We believe that engaging in a sustained process of curricular and pedagogical co-construction will produce more powerful principal preparation programs. *Co-construction* means working together within the richness and against the limitations of multiple knowledge domains to create new knowledge. It means harnessing the knowledge from both systems—the university and the world of practice—and, rather than picking and choosing from that body of knowledge, leveraging it, integrating it, weaving it together and creating powerful learning opportunities where it can be pushed, prodded, and developed even further.

In order to engage in co-construction, participants must develop a deeper knowledge and understanding of each other's systems. University faculties must realize that school districts function as systems with incentive structures, accountability practices, and cultural proclivities. Practitioners must realize the same about universities. However, in this co-constructed relationship, both entities must share the orientation that the preparatory program functions in the service of the school system. A program is only as good as its ability to prepare its participants for the systems in which they will have to operate and navigate, and where, ideally, they will effect positive change.

Co-construction therefore relies on the university professors and district- or school-based practitioners together facing the challenge of effective principal preparation. It requires sustained dialogue grounded in ideas of what principals need to know in order to lead instruction, and what preparatory programs need to do in order to facilitate that knowledge construction. It requires a clear sense of purpose and ownership of the work toward a commonly agreed upon outcome or set of outcomes, related to effective teaching for student learning.

Participation in this co-construction also depends on the ability of parties from both systems to abandon belief structures that might impede the co-creation of new knowledge. For example, professors must abandon the notion that "educators are research subjects" to be culled, sifted through, and reported on in research journals. The idea that those teaching in higher education have greater professional cachet than those teaching in elementary and secondary schools must be challenged. Practitioners must abandon the notion of "professor as expert," which often leads to disappointment and disillusionment when the professor's expertise proves less than useful to a particular practice-based problem. The idea that "professors are parasites," which develops from the feeling among many practitioners that researchers arrive at schools, take data out, contribute very little in return, and write articles that earn them prestige in the research community when their name becomes associated with the exemplary practice of school-based practitioners schools (since "research subjects" must typically remain anonymous), must be challenged.

Central to an authentic, meaningful, and powerful co-constructive model, is the practice of ongoing reflection, transparency of work, and cyclical learning. Co-construction is a continuous process that grows out of relentless, open, and honest conversations between practitioners and professors about how to approach the preparation of future leaders to improve instruction for all students. Together, college faculty and district-level professionals model for aspiring leaders the capacity of a community of learners to face and struggle with hard issues.

To be successful, such programs must be designed to address a series of dichotomies. First, they have to confront the age-old tension between theory and practice. When programs are built upon the belief that implicit in strong practice are deeply-embedded theoretical rationales (Schön 1983), they are more likely to find areas of common ground. They will also be able to challenge the status quo, and produce something new. The co-constructive model is designed to uncover and then mine tacit knowledge held by exemplary practitioners. As faculties collaboratively explore and expose this tacit knowledge, they can convert the day-to-day sense-making behind best leadership practices into teachable points of view (Tichy with Cohen, 1997).

Among the most powerful dimensions of practitioners and professors working together on a consistent basis is that it provides an ongoing opportunity for each group to make itself understood by the other. This need for explanation provides a concrete context and a sense of urgency to engage in reflective professional practice. School practices, university procedures, classroom pedagogy, and habits of mind all become grist with which to deepen collective knowledge about school leadership.

Second, leadership preparation programs must tackle the tension between preparation and practice. This approach posits the relationship between preparatory development and practice as circular rather than linear. Learning for training is learning for practice, and learning for practice is learning for training. Knowledge construction is not static; it is symbiotic. In contrast, traditional preparation models rely on the university to train future principals, based on some combination of the professors' past experiences, the research in which they have engaged, and/or the scholarship of others that they have read. The lessons that result are often based on outdated conceptions of the nature of the principalship and of schooling. In the turbulent world of school reform, we cannot afford the time it takes for new learning to be published and made accessible to future leaders. We need to be able to transfer the learning of practitioners who are currently struggling with the chaotic, and ever changing work on to the next generation of school leaders at an accelerated rate. Programs designed to give educators practice as school leaders at the same time that they are becoming conversant in the theory behind the practice provide them with learning opportunities that incorporate the best practices of working practitioners, as well as the thinking, writing, and reflection on the theoretical framework from which that practice evolved.

Third, powerful preparation programs have the capacity to resolve tensions between professors and practitioners. Although in the field of education professors and practitioners work together on various projects, they often approach their work from very different points of view. Critical to the success of a co-constructive model is the development and articulation of a common understanding about what constitutes effective school leadership. Both partners need to be able to articulate their tacit beliefs and approaches. They need to be able to answer the questions: What skills, knowledge, and habits of mind do school leaders need in order to run schools effectively? How will we know if our programs are successful in developing the necessary skills, knowledge, and habits in future leaders? How will we hold ourselves accountable? The co-constructive model requires practitioners and professors to face these issues together, and to find common ground on which to construct a program powerful enough to prepare educators to lead schools so that all students can reach high levels of academic performance. Together, they must hold the preparatory programs accountable for that which its graduates are accountable: the leading of good teaching for the facilitation of powerful learning. Ultimately, if student performance is the measure of a principal's success, then a preparatory program's success should be measured in the same fashion. Professors and practitioners must agree to evaluate their programs based upon the ability of their graduates to fulfill the mission of the schools and systems in which they operate.

What we are proposing here is a model of co-construction in which practitioners and professors form a unified program faculty, sustain deep and challenging dialogues about preparatory practice, and commit to the continual improvement of the work of preparing future leaders for an ever evolving reality. To that end, university faculties must seek partners who are actively and conscientiously engaged in knowledge production, who are familiar with the professional literature on school leadership, and who can articulate a clear concept of the principal as instructional leader. In like form, practitioners should seek university partners that are flexible, risk-taking, and adept at doing the inductive work of looking at practice and locating it within a useful theoretical framework. University faculties must be committed to the dissemination of knowledge in the service of improved practice, and they must be both willing to part with past practice and eager to experiment with new curricular and pedagogical approaches. Both parties must be committed to ongoing learning about curricular gaps identified by the feedback of district-level employers and program graduates. Both parties must be committed to filling those curricular gaps through new preparatory practice, and both must be willing to build a common vocabulary and culture.

THE QUESTIONS WE ASKED

In preparing ourselves for this engagement, we looked to the experts. In particular, we built our work on the foundation of management literature that advises industries interested in adapting to changes in market conditions to bring the consumer "into the room" (Pinson and Jinnett 1996, 27–41; Bangs 1998). This work suggests that a change in proximity between consumer and service provider can give institutions access to valuable information on the fluctuating needs of the marketplace, and insight into how to go about meeting those needs.

As we contemplated the implications of this strategy for the context in which we were working, we began to ask, who exactly is the consumer of school leadership preparation programs? The university behaved as though their consumers were individual students for whom they competed with other colleges and universities for market share. Their product/program was designed and pitched to attract a niche in that market. In the case of most principal preparation programs in New York City, the niche could be described as: students with full-time jobs who required supervisory certification for career advancement, and were looking for a program that would provide the necessary credits after regular work hours with as much ease as possible. These student characteristics were viable because they were based upon an understanding implicit in the system, that it was the certificate that stood in the way of upward mobility. This understanding was supported by the experience that knowledge and skill, where needed, could be (and usually were) acquired "on-the-job," or through other venues, such as workshops, professional literature, and mentor relationships.

Although most programs were thought to be of limited value by participants and graduates alike, the student body did not demand a change. The pressure came directly from the future employers of those students and through the state on the employers' behalf. As the pressure to improve teaching and accelerate learning increased, superintendents grew acutely aware and increasingly vocal about the problem of middle-management leadership capacity, namely the quality of novice principal leadership as a major stumbling block to school reform. Superintendents pointed out that the succession pipeline was not working well enough to meet the increased demand, either with respect to the number of candidates available to them, or with respect to the quality of those candidates. In addition, the way the current system was designed gave them no direct institutional role from which to influence the nature of the university credentialing process, and/or what that process produced—candidates for principalships. Superintendents were being held more and more accountable for the quality of instruction in their schools, and the academic achievement of their students. However, it was the university, sanctioned by the state, that was responsible for providing principal candidates with the baseline knowledge and skill with which they were supposed to do their job.

The logic of this inquiry soon led to another question, how does a university faculty know if it is running a "quality" program? How does the university know if the program does what it is supposed to do? And yet another question, what *is* the university supposed to do?

One relatively common way to evaluate the success of a preparatory program is to look at the employability of its graduates, and the degree of satisfaction reported by the primary employer(s). Employability presents a problem, however, when there is an acute labor shortage and most program graduates can secure jobs. The more powerful question—does the program do what it is supposed to do well enough to satisfy the employer?—redefines the consumer of the university's services, and in so doing, identifies who needs to be invited "into the room" as a partner.

Once the consumer was re-defined as the employer, and the partner was redefined as the district, a reciprocal system of accountability could be developed. The employer/district could hold the university accountable for the quality of its product/graduates. In exchange, the university would receive information about how to determine who should be admitted to school leadership preparation programs, what aspiring leaders should know and be able to do before they graduate, and insight into how to measure whether or not that knowledge and skill has been mastered. In addition, this partnership could provide the college with access to schools in which aspiring leaders could observe and learn from the work of expert practitioners, as well as opportunities for them to apply their emergent skills to real tasks under the supervision and support of professionals with a real stake in their learning. Finally, it would give the university a competitive edge by providing access to information about the school system and the realities of school leadership in ways that would allow for programmatic responsiveness and increased demand for a quality curriculum.

Once the consumer was "in the room," another set of questions emerged. What body of knowledge and skills could a school leadership preparatory program reasonably be expected to address, and what should it include in the domain of inservice training and support? And, what should the responsibility of the district in developing high quality school leadership be? In the absence of a meaningful relationship such as this, these questions had been ignored.

The relationship set in motion an iterative process of inquiry. District superintendents wanted the program to reflect their instructional approach; they wanted candidates for school leadership positions to enter their districts already acculturated. Was there, for example, some generic set of knowledge and skills that all school leaders needed to master that could be transformed into curriculum for the preparatory program, leaving the culture-specific work for the district on-the-job training and support systems to address? Was the cultural border to be considered *the* border between preservice and inservice school leadership development? How exactly would that work? Could we separate the teaching of leadership skills from specific content? Inspired by the literature on knowledge construction and acquisition (Berns and Erickson 2001; Borko and Putnam 1998; Brown and Palincsar 1989; Piaget 1929; Resnick and Hall 1998; Resnick and Nelson-Le Gall 1997) we wondered how aspiring leaders would go about constructing the knowledge and acquiring the leadership skills they needed, separate from gaining mastery over the contextually-driven content. Even if it was possible, could it be done without watering down the preparatory curriculum so much that it would be of little use when graduates finally came face-to-face with real circumstances in the schools? It became evident that to strike a balance between the demand for preparatory program rigor and the desire to design a program that appealed to as many consumers/employers as possible, universities would have to make a choice. They would have to define a market niche—this time, based upon the characteristics of the customer/employer rather than those of the consumer/student. In order to be successful, the university would have to select a group of partners with "similar enough" instructional approaches, and it would have to design a program around what those districts had in common.

Once the university and the district/employer were in "partnership," we faced the challenge of coming from two distinct institutional cultures—that of the university and that of the school district, that of the professor and that of the practitioner. Our first task was to agree on a set of core beliefs that would guide and be reflected in every decision to be made. The program was built on four common understandings about schooling:

- First, *the purpose of school leadership is to improve instruction.* The evidence of instructional improvement resides in the quality of student work.

- Second, *the greatest predictor of student learning is the quality of the teaching a student receives* (National Commission on Teaching and America's Future 1996; Sanders and Horn 1994; Sanders, Saxton, and Horn 1998). The most powerful pathway to the improvement of teaching is through adult learning.

Future school leaders must therefore learn to organize schools for the adult learning required to enhance student learning.

- Third, *one cannot lead what one does not know.* In order to lead adults in their instructional practices, a school leader must have experiential knowledge of powerful instructional practices. Although there may be generic principles for good leadership, at its core, leadership is driven by context. The leadership of student and adult teaching and learning therefore requires deep and thorough knowledge of effective instructional practices, as well as knowledge of how these approaches work in a variety of educational contexts.

- Fourth, *schools and districts are organizational systems.* Efforts at improvement must therefore be approached systematically. Leaders need to know how to use all of the institutional structures and functions available to them in order to organize and manage them so that they are focused on their instructional goals.

With these beliefs as our foundation, we could face and bridge the cultural divide.

CO-CONSTRUCTION

Co-construction is a complex process. In order for participants with diverse training and experience to create something new together, something that each takes ownership of and actively supports, the work must be anchored in common ground. Finding that common ground is particularly challenging when the partnership involves participants from social institutions with very different cultural norms and incentive structures. Once we got past the usual platitudes—of which the commonly stated belief that "All children can learn" or "Good leaders know how to collaborate" are emblematic—into the nitty-gritty of the *what, how, when,* and *why* of the work we found ourselves facing our differences.

What evolved was a nonlinear, messy way of working that went something like this. We did or *tried* to do something together, such as designing a learning experience to teach aspiring leaders a particular leadership strategy; and, in the process of trying to do it, we exposed what we believed. Individual beliefs evolved into shared beliefs in the *doing*, as we worked through the details of designing the learning experience. Once identified and articulated, shared beliefs could then be used to reflect on and evaluate our curricular and pedagogical decisions. Our emergent, shared belief system thereby created a tie that bound the parts of the program into a coherent whole.

Quite frankly, we came to this way of working with some reluctance. On the surface, it seemed much more sensible to identify common beliefs, values, and vision first and then do the work of transforming these shared understandings into teachable behaviors and habits of mind. What we found was that when our agreements were not crafted in *the doing*, they deteriorated into a string of words that we did not uphold. Inevitably, our vision and values were revealed not through what we said, but through what we did.

To the extent that we discovered or uncovered a reliable compass by which to orient our work, it was the accountability model we had adopted. Our model prompted us to ask and to answer over and over the question: Why do aspiring leaders need to know this content and be able to do this activity? If the content (knowledge and skill) and the pedagogy used to master it could not be linked directly to what the employer expected novice principals to be able to do, we were compelled to ask: Why should we include it? No matter how worthwhile that knowledge, perspective, or approach might be for other purposes, if we could not answer our own questions about it, we left it outside of the scope of the preparatory program.

It was remarkable (at least to us) how profoundly this orientation affected our work. It literally shaped the content. The language the employers and expert practitioners used to describe the competencies of novice principals was the language of behaviors. They talked about what principals did. And, they talked about what they had to know in order to do it. Their language reflected how principals figured out what to do in response to changes or circumstances in the environment in which they worked. The district wanted the program to evoke desired behaviors and habitual ways of thinking so that the actions of program graduates could be trusted and relied upon once they became novice principals.

This perspective informed our pedagogy. Inspired by the literature on adult learning (Bransford, Brown, and Cocking 1999; Comings, Garner, and Smith 2000; Knowles 1980), we had to create learning opportunities for future principals that involved them in the doing (rather than listening to talk about the doing). The doing had to be shaped around tasks that aspiring leaders were expected to perform as novice principals, and it had to provide adequate practice in both analyzing new environments and responding to them, so that the work could become habitual, trustworthy, and reliable.

All this focus on practice raised the question of the role of the university. Were we really just talking about an apprenticeship model in which novices learn their craft under the tutelage of expert practitioners? Could, or should, school districts petition the state to assume the role of credentialing their employees? What did, or should, the professor contribute to the preparatory process? What the practitioners brought "into the room" was expertise based upon their collective past experience and new insights gained as a result of individual experimentation in response to specific circumstances. The skills in which the expert practitioner was versed were relatively reliable in contexts that resembled those they had encountered in the past. The problem was that those environments were becoming less and less predictable. The professors were skilled at placing the practitioners' expertise into a theoretical framework. So placed, it became a set of steps to guide practitioners through unfamiliar territory: (a) Make visible the logic of next steps, (b) Anticipate the action of others, (c) Identify pathways to new knowledge development, and (d) Link and integrate what is known to the new learning. Ronald Heifetz and Marty Linsky (2002) use the image of the balcony and the dance floor. They advise leaders to occupy both spaces moving back and forth between participant and observer: to act, on the dance floor, moving in response to one's partner and the other dancers; and to gain perspective, to contemplate the action, and to figure out how all the parties are dancing

17

from the balcony. It was precisely because the professors were not practitioners, that they could and did ask not only *what* and *how* but *why* practitioners did what they did. And then, more and more, *why* did they (the practitioners) do *this* instead of *that*? What did they see in the environment that clued their behavior? The deeper the questioning went, the more patterns emerged; this was the logic of theory. The more the theory emerged, the deeper the questioning; we were mining practice for what was teachable through the program.

This approach, of course, raised the question of what was and was not "teachable." What was nurture and what was nature? Could the program be expected to make leaders? Did everyone have the capacity to be a leader and if they did, could they become leaders in the time we had to prepare them for school leadership? If we were only going to prepare those who we had a reasonable chance of turning into leaders within the time we had to prepare them, how would we know who they were? Certainly the university's standard screening process through an admissions committee judging paper applications was not sensitive enough to be reliable. The districts knew the candidates from their own schools. What should their role be in determining who was admitted to the program? If we depended only upon the judgment of the participating districts, how would we know if that judgment was a fair and equitable one?

We worked the issues through without the luxury of having "enough time." (As Peter Senge, Kleiner, Roberts, Ross, Roth, and Smith [1999] point out, there is never "enough time.") This condition forced us to acknowledge that the work we were doing was not once-and-for-all-time work. It was ongoing and would need to be done over and over again. Furthermore, the two-way accountability relationship between the partners prompted us to confront what we came to call the "rhetoric-reality gap": the difference between what we said and what we did. In response, we had to craft new approaches to deal with and respond to the unintended consequences of what we taught and how we taught it, and we had to adopt some platitudes or our own: "Stick-to-itiveness works" and "Incremental change counts."

Among things that changed as a result of this work was each partner's investment strategy. The district's role in program admission prompted them to search systematically to find leadership potential—people in whom they were willing to invest time and money. When the first crop of aspiring leaders had been exhausted, the district was motivated to invest in opportunities to cultivate leadership potential—future entrants to the program. In addition, involvement in the content and pedagogy of the program clarified the district's role in providing ongoing inservice leadership development and support, and mobilized investment in it. From these investments, a functional school leadership pipeline began to emerge.

The challenge the university faced was that its institutional incentives favored resistance to change. Even in the face of the enthusiastic support of the program by administrators, tenured faculty members were under no formal obligation to alter what and how they were teaching or to put time and energy into co-constructing a new program. The most prudent pathway for the university administration to take in order to leverage the change they wanted was to engage, support, and invest in untenured faculty who were not as accustomed to traditional ways of doing things. Over time, this strategy had the potential to act as a catalyst for changing the university's cultural norms. However, untenured faculty members were also under considerable pressure to publish their work in scholarly journals.

The university had become more invested in the success of the participating districts in general and the graduates of the program in particular. The ongoing relationship with the district gave professors access to information about how graduates were coping with the day-to-day challenges of the principalship, as well as insight into what components of the program they found useful and not so useful on-the-job. The university became invested in a different definition of success for program graduates and faculty alike. The indicator by which it based its evaluation of the program and its faculty came to reflect how well graduates performed as novice principals. Professors grew invested in bringing as many aspiring leaders in the program as they could to high levels of on-the-job performance through a continuous cycle of accountable program improvement. This approach required a nontraditional pedagogy.

THE PEDAGOGY

The Traditional Classroom

Imagine entering a classroom at a local university. Standing at the front of the room are Professor Enid Larz and Principal Joan Leigh. Dr. Larz is describing the need for distributive leadership in schools. She explains that the most recent literature provides a model of distributed leadership that involves collaborative decision making, trust, and shared accountability. Reviewing the work of Spillane, Halverson, and Diamond (2001), which the course participants read for that night's class, Dr. Larz describes theories of distributed cognition and activity theory. She draws a model of individuals working within environments, using arrows that indicate "sense-making" between the individuals and the contexts in which they work. She describes the tools of leadership practice, and illustrates how various tools require teachers to think differently about the task of teaching. When she is done reviewing the article, she turns to Ms. Leigh, her co-teacher, and sits down. Ms. Leigh steps forward and explains how she talks with each of her faculty members after she observes a lesson. She describes a recent situation in which one of the fourth grade teachers at her school prepared an excellent lesson on fractions. Ms. Leigh recalls for the class how after reviewing the lesson with the teacher, she asked whether the teacher would be interested in taking on a leadership role in math education. Ms. Leigh then describes the teacher's excitement at being asked to serve in that capacity, and her anticipated success at getting other teachers to alter their math instruction. As the professor and principal talk, the students take notes, occasionally asking questions or offering comments. What is wrong with this picture?

In this vignette, the professor and practitioner provide future leaders with important information in a way that is inconsistent with the information they are trying to provide. They employ a pedagogy that assumes that adults learn through listening, that knowledge is transmissable from one person to another through talk, and that adults can recall information told to them months (and even years) earlier, and put it to good use. Their assumptions about learning, which are inconsistent with the theory and practice they are trying to impart, may or may not be explicit to them. Their way of teaching, however, is traditional and grounded in years of educational experience at the university level. Traditional preparatory programs for school leaders provide learning opportunities based on the assumption that knowledge can be acquired outside of the actual need for that knowledge, and recalled later when it is needed in practice. They also assume that knowledge is given through talking and received through listening (for a similar argument, see Bridges and Hallinger 1995, 4–5).

Every pedagogical approach rests on a series of assumptions about how people learn. By making such assumptions about learning theories explicit, program faculty can discern not only *what* future leaders should learn but also *how* future leaders should learn. If all parties agree that the role of pedagogy in a preparatory program is to facilitate the relevant learning that practitioners will need, professors and practitioners can then come together to co-construct the form that relevant learning opportunities for future leaders should take. The literature on adult learning can inform that co-construction.

Adult learning theory tells us that powerful learning happens through doing, and that adults can most easily remember any knowledge that they put to immediate use (Bransford, Brown, and Cocking 1999; Comings, Garner, and Smith 2000; Knowles 1980). Based on this theory, we believe that when adults participate in learning opportunities in which they solve problems, trigger and incorporate prior knowledge, and reflect critically on their problem-solving practices, they engage in a process of constructing the new knowledge that they will need when they encounter similar problems in the future. Given that theory, then, how should professors and practitioners co-construct more relevant and more powerful learning opportunities for future school leaders? How can they create conditions in which future leaders will develop the school leadership equivalent of "muscle memory"?—a set of guiding pedagogical principles can orient that work.

The work of training future principals should be embedded in the actual job of leading a school. Since we are training leaders to work in specific organizational systems, we must determine what responsibilities those systems will hold school leaders accountable for and give future principals many opportunities to practice meeting those responsibilities. For example, if the school system our program serves holds principals accountable for leading adults in their instructional practice so that students meet performance standards, we have to figure out how to provide aspiring leaders with opportunities to analyze student performance data, to determine whether students are meeting standards, and to figure out what the student performance data and classroom observations tell us about what a given teacher needs to learn. We have to craft the appropriate simulations so that they can practice analyzing actual student assessment data in relation to teacher capacity and develop strategies to foster that capacity, so that their strategies become habituated.

The role of the instructors, then, is to determine the relevant learning opportunities that future leaders need, and to provide those opportunities. In this way, instructors serve as facilitators of knowledge construction, rather than as imparters of knowledge. They design the appropriate exercises and activities that allow for the generation of new knowledge among aspiring leaders. Paradoxically, the most time-consuming work of the instructor, then, lies outside the actual class meeting. It involves the analysis of the daily demands on the principal, and the design of relevant activities in which aspiring leaders can practice responding to those demands. It also involves identifying appropriate research-based resources to help them to think about how to respond to those demands, and providing opportunities for them to reflect on their responses through conversations and individual feedback.

PROGRAM ACCOUNTABILITY

Although we live in an era of standards-based accountability for schools, only recently have discussions about holding university programs accountable for their effectiveness in preparing school leaders surfaced. Aside from traditional mechanisms of program accreditation through state review, which vary from state to state, preparatory programs are not held accountable for the leaders they produce. It is therefore important to frame the context for our accountability agreements within the broader context of principal preparatory program accountability.

In the mid-1990s, the Interstate School Leaders Licensure Consortium (ISLLC) produced and distributed a series of six standards for school leaders. These standards are all grounded in the concept that a principal promotes student success by having a specific knowledge base, a certain set of beliefs and attitudes, and an ability to engage in activities and processes with a school community. One of the presumed uses of the ISLLC standards is to shape preparation programs for school leaders. To that end, the standards themselves and a paper entitled *Using ISLLC Standards to Strengthen Preparation Programs in School Administration* (Van Meter and Murphy 1997) were disseminated to various universities that offer such programs. Individual states and school districts reviewed those standards; adapted, revised and expanded upon them; and then distributed them to schools. The ISLLC standards, although grounded in student learning as the ultimate goal of school leadership, are not intended to measure the work of university programs in preparing school leaders. Although theoretically they help to anchor programs in student performance, they do not provide any mechanisms for holding preparatory programs accountable.

Since the systemic work of holding preparatory programs accountable is in its embryonic stage at the state and national levels, co-constructed programs have to create clear mechanisms for evaluating and responding to programs currently in use in partnership with local school districts. Indeed, when universities and districts collaborate to co-construct preparatory programs, they enter into a relationship of reciprocal accountability. The districts, as the employers of program graduates, hold the universities accountable for training effective leaders in powerful and meaningful ways. They do so as consumers of this service. If they are not satisfied with a university's performance in co-constructing the curriculum, its responsiveness to local educational practice, or the effectiveness of the program, they can take their business elsewhere (provided that there is another university close by). Certainly in urban areas, there are many universities from which to choose, providing the districts with an exit option that should motivate university faculty to respond to district needs.

As participants in the co-construction of the program, districts can also hold the university accountable. If districts identify gaps in the training of program graduates once they are on the job, they are in a position to add elements to the program to fill those gaps. In turn, the university can hold the district accountable for the support and guidance needed to develop a powerful program, including access to schools for site visits, student performance data, teacher observation exercises, and other learning opportunities for program participants. Because university faculty are trained in the systematic evaluation of program effectiveness, they can contribute their expertise in designing evaluations to determine a program's success with both formative and summative measures. In this system of reciprocal accountability between the university and the district, the two entities must come together to ask fundamental questions about precisely how and for what the preparatory program should be held accountable.

We believe that improved student performance is the ultimate measure of a preparatory program's effectiveness. We see the students' performance (measured in multiple ways) as an indicator of teacher performance, and the teacher's performance as an indicator of the school leader's performance, and the leader's performance as an indicator of the preparatory program's performance at preservice training, as well as an indicator of the district's effectiveness at providing inservice training. Although we are confident in the logic that traces student performance back through leadership preparation, we are less certain about how to determine the appropriate time frame for evaluating a preparatory program's success through student performance, what precise measures of local accountability we should use in the meantime, and how to account for the varied and diverse political contexts in which school leaders operate.

More precisely, if we believe that university preparatory programs should be held accountable for their graduates' abilities to improve student learning through the development of effective instructional practices, we need to discern how long we think it should reasonably take for programs to know whether or not they are effective. This task is daunting. How long does it take for a school leader to improve instruction? How long does it take for student learning to reflect improved instruction? On what measures of student learning should we base our evaluations of our program's success? Unfortunately, we have not been in the business of co-constructed preparatory programs long enough to be able to discern whether our programs are effective in sustainable ways.

Given the challenges of determining the time it takes to improve student performance, we believe that programs engaged in leadership preparation can develop intermediate accountability practices that involve school districts and communities. These local accountability practices allow for continual programmatic improvement through reflection and systematic observation of what program graduates tend to know and not know as they assume leadership positions.

Introducing Intermediate Accountability

Through a process of formative reflection, constant dialogue, and periodic readjustment, local accountability mechanisms provide a continual feedback loop for preparatory programs. Intermediate accountability practices include gathering feedback from the graduates' employers (the school districts in which they work), and feedback from the graduates themselves once they are on the job.

At the district level, the superintendents and deputy superintendents hold principals accountable by observing their work during school site visits (in which teachers' instructional practices are observed), in professional development activities for school leaders, and in parent and community feedback. Superintendents know when school leaders are floundering and when they are performing at high levels because of their network of contacts within the district system. By identifying patterns in their observations of new leaders, they also know whether there might be a problem with an individual's fit with a given school, an individual's competence, or a pattern that represents a gap in the training that recent program graduates have received. When a gap in training is identified, the district and university faculty members need to discuss how to fill that gap, where in the curriculum's scope and sequence it might be addressed, and how to create appropriate learning opportunities to ensure that future graduates do not face the same challenges unprepared.

Similarly, program graduates are an important resource for holding preparatory programs accountable. These graduates know firsthand what they feel prepared to do and what they find daunting and overwhelming in their early years on the job. Through continual conversations, participation as course instructors or visitors, and surveys, program graduates can provide a wealth of information about where a program is doing well and where it is falling short in training school leaders. Program graduates should be recognized as those with the most recent and concrete knowledge of the program's effectiveness, and their experiences mined for any indication of a program's gaps in training.

Accounting for Contexts

Since program graduates confront varied and diverse contexts once they assume leadership positions, the accountability mechanisms must be flexible and responsive to the various school and community environments. What needs to emerge is a model in which the value added of a new leader can be accounted for, whether that added value is grounded in measures of student performance, parent satisfaction, or improved teacher practice. For example, if a recent program graduate assumes a leadership position at a high-performing school where parents have exhibited considerable dissatisfaction with a series of principals, how should she be held accountable? Since student performance has always been high there, we would want her to maintain and develop the instructional practice of the effective teachers as well as focus on students, however few of them there may be who are struggling to come to standards. We would also, however, want to hold her accountable for understanding and responding to the community, and the culture of the school. If another program graduate assumed a leadership role in a school with minimal parental involvement, less effective instruction, and lower student performance, we would want to tailor accountability measures to fit that context. A preparatory program can only know its effectiveness if it knows the contexts for which it is preparing future leaders, and the leaders' ability to function effectively in those contexts.

Using Reciprocal Accountability

In the structures created through co-constructed preparatory programs, accountability becomes another form of respect and reciprocity. University faculty members are commonly hired to conduct large- and small-scale evaluations of professional practice, resources for sound evaluation design can be leveraged from both the university and district systems. Both the university and the district can use observed patterns in leadership performance, teacher performance, and student performance at schools led by program graduates to determine what parts of the program serve students well and what parts need to grow or change. As school-based realities, school governance structures, and education policies are constantly evolving, so too should the preparatory programs evolve. The districts and universities need to construct mechanisms to hold each other accountable for continual learning, adapting, and improving upon the preparatory program to train leaders for the dynamic, complex, and chaotic reality of public school leadership.

CHAPTER TWO

THE THEORY IN PRACTICE
OUR STORY

To return to our relationship theme, we would now like to give the reader a sense of how the theory espoused in the preceding section played itself out in real life: the issues that arose; the compromises that were made; the agreements that emerged; and the products that the process produced. Through our story, we hope to show our appreciation for the inevitable gap between our "theory *of* practice" and the "theory *in* practice" (Argyris 1986, 1991; Argyris and Schön 1974; Schön 1983, 1987). Anyone who has been in a relationship knows all too well that there is the romantic Hollywood ideal, on the one hand, and the reality of day-to-day relating, negotiating, and compromising on the other. In this section, we extract from our experience some guiding principles or lessons about choosing institutional partners for collaborative work. Although we do not imagine other districts or universities to have identical circumstances to ours, we do think that there are universal lessons to be learned from our particular relationship.

THE DISTRICT'S TALE

In 1987, when Anthony Alvarado became superintendent of Community School District Two in New York City, the district ranked tenth in reading and mathematics out of the city's thirty-two community school districts. By 1996, it ranked second. As Richard

Elmore and Deanna Burney (1997) point out, "These gains occurred during a time in which the number of immigrant students in the district increased and the student population grew more linguistically diverse and economically poor. Many of the immigrants entering school came with less education and linguistic development than had previously been the case" (6).

Central to Alvarado's approach to reform was a decentralized strategy for instructional improvement. In order for this approach to work, he needed principals in the district to understand that principal leadership was a matter of improving instruction. And he had to be able to hire and retain principals based upon their willingness and ability to accept and act upon this notion. As Elmore with Burney (1997) discuss, Alvarado saw "the principalship as the linchpin of his systemic strategy," and he understood that if he could not influence which people became principals in the district, he could not decentralize and get the results he wanted. Alvarado and his staff focused "what would be seen in most school systems as an inordinate amount of attention on recruitment of principals, on the grooming of emerging leaders within the district for principalships, on the creation of support networks for acting and probationary principals, and on the creation of norms that principals are to participate along with teachers in staff-development activities dealing with content-focused instruction" (27).

During Alvarado's first four years in District Two, he replaced approximately two-thirds of the sitting principals (Elmore with Burney 1997). Some retired, some moved to other districts. After the initial turnover of incumbents who did not support the reform strategy, Alvarado faced an even more insidious problem, that of so-called principal brain drain due to competition with other districts in the marketplace. A combination of inadequacies in the New York City supervisory union contract and the district's growing reputation for strong instructional leadership made District Two a prime target for recruitment by surrounding suburban districts that could afford to offer principals higher salaries, as well as more favorable working conditions. Confronted with the economic reality that there wasn't much difference in pay between a principal and a teacher at the top of the scale, taking into account differences in the contractual hours worked per day and the degree of difficulty in the job of principal, many principals who supported Alvarado's reform agenda were enticed to leave District Two for jobs elsewhere.

New York City employs a two-step principal selection process. Local school committees recommend candidates to the superintendent, and the superintendent makes appointments from among those recommended. The quality of Alvarado's principal appointments was limited by the quality of the candidates recommended to him by the schools. The district had employed a search-and-find strategy to identify potential candidates compatible with its approach to reform. Networks of practitioners at all levels of the organization were mobilized to locate promising principal leadership potential, both within and outside of the district, and to recruit them as applicants for the principal selection process. The tenacity with which the district employed this strategy soon gained them a reputation of being somewhat predatory. However, over time, the strategy became less and less productive and the pool from which schools were obliged to make their recommendations became increasingly stale. The process began to churn up the same names over and over and the district frequently faced a choice between postponing a principal appointment and selecting someone who was not really a good match for the school or the district. The situation was further exacerbated by the fact that the district did not have a pool of assistant principals, already acculturated to the district, from which to draw. As a way of redirecting resources to their professional development effort, administrative positions at the district and school levels had been cut dramatically. What little administrative support remained at the school level was in the form of administrative assistants. The administrative assistant position was not an appointed title, and as such did not require supervisory certification. That is, it could and usually was, filled by a teacher on out-of-classroom assignment. While the job proved to be a way for teachers to explore their emergent interest in becoming supervisors, they needed to complete supervisory certification requirements before they could become candidates for principal vacancies. If the district chose to look into the future, the picture became even gloomier. In addition to the ongoing brain drain, a large number of strong veteran principals were expected to leave the district within a short period of time, as they reached retirement age. It seemed clear that something had to be done.

The district decided to try to "grow its own," that is, to identify teachers with leadership potential who were acculturated to the districtwide approach to teaching and learning, and to fund their supervisory certification process. However, if the district was going to make such an investment in its future leadership workforce, it wanted the program responsible for preparing supervisors for certification to reflect the districtwide instructional belief system. Central to that belief system was the critical role of the principal in improving instruction.

The district was not authorized by the state to run its own preparatory program. Although it was an intriguing idea to petition the state for that authority, given the urgency of the need and the political difficulties such a petition would entail, it did not seem prudent to pursue this avenue. The district needed to partner with a credit-granting entity—a university—if it wanted to grow its own. It needed to find a university that was familiar with the districtwide reform strategy, one that was responsive to what the district thought aspiring principals needed to know and able to participate in and contribute to that strategy.

The district had many relationships with universities within the geographical area. Along with outside consultants and internal professional developers, universities and their faculties had played a critical role in supporting the district's approach to professional learning for teachers. Alvarado, and his then Deputy Superintendent Elaine Fink, decided to partner with one of these universities.

The dean of education of the university they selected was enthusiastic and pledged to give the experiment her full support. She and the superintendent agreed in principle upon a program of study that would be co-taught by a university professor and a district principal/practitioner, and that would reflect the district's values and beliefs about instruction and leadership for instructional improvement. However, what began as a marriage-made-in-heaven soon fell apart at both the administrative and program delivery levels. University professors resisted working collaboratively with principal/practitioners. Courses continued to be taught in a lecture format, and the content remained unchanged. The program was organized around what the professors knew (and therefore could teach), rather than around an agreed upon set of practical competencies aspiring leaders needed to master. There was little or no coordination between classes, with different professors sometimes giving the same assigned reading. Reading materials were often based upon outdated research. Few of those teaching in the program had any experience in schools, and those who had such experience had not been in classrooms for a very long time. However, no overt conflict erupted. Faculty resistance to the agreed upon arrangement was passive (e.g., phone calls to arrange co-teaching and planning schedules not returned). It remains unclear how aware university administrators were of the problems as they occurred. In their defense, university incentive structures in general provide university deans with very little power to influence what tenured faculty teach and how they teach it. As a result, the district ended the relationship after one year.

As with all failed relationships, the experience taught the district some important lessons. First, it was necessary, but not sufficient, for the district to have the approval and support of the university administration. In addition, university faculty members teaching the courses had to embrace the idea of the program if the collaborative relationship was to work. Second, it was not possible to exaggerate the administrative nightmare created by two large institutions trying to forge a new relationship; everyone needed to be prepared for everything to go wrong that could go wrong, and to have a sense of humor about it.

In addition, the district became much clearer about what it wanted out of a collaborative relationship; and some of what it wanted was nonnegotiable (here again, the rules of dating apply: Know what is and is not important to you!). The district knew it needed to play an active role in shaping the preparatory course of study—both its content and its pedagogy. At the core of Alvarado's reform strategy was an investment in and focus on teacher and principal professional development (see Elmore with Burney 1997). As a result, the district had accumulated a wealth of knowledge and experience concerning powerful models of adult learning. Furthermore, years of successful, sustained focus on achieving higher levels of student performance through higher levels of professional performance had produced a coherent body of knowledge that the district believed professionals needed to master. That body of knowledge was reflected in the "work-tasks" that Alvarado and Deputy Elaine Fink expected principals to perform in order to lead instructional improvement. In their experience, those tasks were best mastered in the doing; that is, through authentic, experientially based, job-embedded learning processes. These included extensive opportunities to practice skills, and tasks, and to receive informed feedback on their practice.

Like all romantic tales, there is a bit of mystery surrounding the story of how Alvarado and Fink came to pay a call on Baruch College of the City University of New York. Certainly there was an institutional relationship to build upon. In the past, Baruch and District Two had collaborated in the creation of a high school located on the Baruch campus. In order to make that happen, a panoply of administrative issues had to find successful pathways to resolution through the medieval maze of the university and district bureaucracies. That history boded well for any administrative nightmares that might arise, and the players were known to one another, at least at the higher organizational levels. Still, Baruch was not an obvious choice. Among other things, it did not have a school of education. The School of Education had been dissolved, and the public and education administration programs had been moved to the newly formed School of Public Affairs. Senior education professors associated with the school Administration and Supervision program had left the college and had been replaced by a small group of untenured faculty.

Sandra Stein was one of those untenured faculty members, fresh from Stanford University and new to the city. She recalls that she was invited to participate in the initial meeting between the university and the district. Led by Fink and Alvarado, the conversation began with a discussion about the focus or purpose of a principal preparatory program. Acting Dean of the School of Public Affairs Carroll Seron explained the school's emphasis on management skills—an area in which the school and college had considerable expertise. Her reasoning was not dissimilar to the reasoning of school boards that have experimented with employing non-educators as superintendents. According to this approach, the principalship is a "middle-management" problem and thereby susceptible to middle-management solutions. Characteristically, the district argued vehemently that the principalship was about "instruction and only instruction" (see Elmore with Burney 1997)—an area in which the district had considerable expertise. According to this approach a supervisory preparatory program for principals should focus on leadership—instructional leadership.

Stein recollects responding to the potential gap in approaches by saying: "I understand that you want to build everything around instructional leadership. I can lead a good graduate-level course. I teach using problem-based and experiential learning. But, I do not know if I am doing enough to develop instructional leadership. I'm going to need help with that." As Stein remembers it, Alvarado replied: "I have to tell you how refreshing it is that you are actually telling me what you don't know. That's promising." Acting Dean Seron suggested that a model employed by the college's executive MPA program, in which professors and practitioners co-teach courses, be used for the principal preparation program, and Alvarado and Fink enthusiastically agreed to the idea. But Alvarado had already heard what he needed to hear Stein's remark: "Here is what I know; here is what I know I don't know." Coming from a member of the faculty who would be teaching in the program, this signaled for him that the relationship he hoped for was possible.

THE UNIVERSITY'S TALE

The School of Public Affairs (SPA) was established at Baruch College of the City University of New York in 1994 by the then College President Matthew Goldstein, now Chancellor of the City University of New York. SPA is the only school of public affairs in the City University (CUNY) and the only publicly-funded school of public affairs in the City of New York.

It was initiated principally to create a more effective vehicle to fulfill the College's historic mission to serve the needs of government (and later, nonprofit) organizations as well as the business community. According to David Birdsell, the executive director of academic programs (similar to an associate dean), and one of the faculty founders of the SPA, a faculty commission convened shortly after

Goldstein became president recommended the creation of SPA in order to better align the program's resources with its mission, attract more attention to public affairs and provide more effective academic and community programs.

According to Birdsell, there was a widely held belief that that "mission had been somewhat obscured by the aggregation of public administration under the aegis of the Business School. Recruitment services and support structures oriented toward getting graduate students into MBA programs tilted toward a very different clientele and arguably a different set of outcomes from the students the college wanted to attract to the MPA program." Many of the college's public administration students were already employed by public-sector and nonprofit agencies in which they sought advancement through the acquisition of a higher degree. They complained that an emphasis on commercial practices siphoned attention away from what they felt they needed to learn in order to be prepared for the jobs they aspired to do.

An example of the disjuncture between business and public administration was the required course in computer systems—an introduction to general information management. Every case studied in the course was a business example. Students felt that exclusive attention to bottom-line problems bore little relation to the information system challenges or budget constraints they would be facing on the job in governmental and not-for-profit settings. They and their employers wanted a program that drew lessons from the private sector, but accounted for programs driven by mission and service rather than by profit alone.

The creation of SPA enabled a more thoroughgoing dialogue between business administration and public administration. By creating a school explicitly devoted to public affairs and public policy, the founders hoped to attract high quality people to the banner of public service and, over time, to assert an influence on how governmental and not-for-profit agencies conducted themselves in the City of New York.

Central to the effort was Goldstein's belief in the power of interdisciplinary work. According to Stan Altman, dean of SPA, Goldstein "thought that by forcing disciplines to work together an intellectual tension was produced at their interfaces that sparked a kind of creativity that didn't happen when people only worked within their own disciplines." This thinking was applied to the issue of public sector professional preparation in SPA's executive programs. Goldstein and the school's founding faculty hoped to evoke a kind of synergy between practice and research in the field of public administration, and thereby provoke the invention of innovative solutions to address public and not-for-profit sector problems. They wanted to try and move beyond simply awarding degrees to qualified candidates. Using the professional preparation programs as a vehicle, the college wanted to play a role in helping to make municipal government and not-for-profit agencies work.

There was a long tradition at Baruch of building partnerships that bridged academia and public agencies. The college wanted to consider the notion that these types of partnerships might be more likely to take hold if program faculty understood sector problems through the eyes of those on the inside—the various governmental and not-for-profit organizations. To run a successful preparatory program and influence how government and not-for-profits worked, faculty would have to understand what those agencies needed to make themselves work—the specific attributes of human capital required to carry out the job; and, they would have to organize the executive program's professional preparatory curriculum around those needs. Collaborative relationships with public-sector agencies and their practitioners could provide this information. Based upon these relationships, college faculty could then figure out how to integrate theory and practice in the disciplines they taught. That is, professors could become responsible for making the translation of the material they taught from classroom to workplace. Under this design, the students would no longer be left to figure out for themselves how to take what they learned at the college and use it on-the-job. However, to do so, a standard curriculum package would no longer be adequate. The curriculum would, to a certain extent, have to be customized to meet the needs of particular public sectors.

In effect, designers of SPA's executive programs were entertaining the notion of a different type of client base. Rather than focusing on individual students, faculty members were considering orienting their programs toward sector agencies as customer/consumer. The Aspiring Leaders Program was a pioneering effort to launch such a niche marketing strategy—identifying a public sector and designing a professional preparatory program oriented toward meeting that sector's human resource needs. Within this model, it would no longer be acceptable for students to learn whatever they learned and then leave. Ideally, what students learned would be shaped in collaboration with the constituent groups with whom the college developed working relationships. Usefulness in the workplace would become both an organizing principle for programs and an indicator of their success. By redefining public sector employers as the customer, orienting the program to meet their needs, and determining success through customer satisfaction, SPA was, in addition, developing a performance outcome approach to holding programs publicly accountable. This perspective represented a profound shift in the academic paradigm. Its implications would, to some degree, transfer to other executive programs run by the school.

SPA was designed to run on a shoestring; it has no unit chairs; and little in the way of release time for administrative services. As a result, according to Birdsell, virtually everything SPA does involves having people work "out of position." In a way, the school's management structure mirrors its interdisciplinary focus. Everyone gets involved in everything.

In order for SPA to work, it has been necessary to find ways to validate collaborative work with the institutions with whom it is partnered as a contribution, rather than a distraction from academic appointments. The administration understands that if SPA is asking junior faculty to teach in a model that requires them to do more work than the traditional one, to attune their classes to the needs of the client, and to sustain innovative programming consistently, they will not be able to publish as much. The research projects they will engage in are likely to be more collaborative than individual, more applied than purely theoretical, and fewer in number by the time they reach their tenure decisions, unless adjustments are made in teaching loads. While they are firmly committed to the production of high-quality scholarship, the SPA administration believes that promotional criteria must evolve to recognize the importance of engaged scholarship and pedagogy, and the time that it takes to accomplish. This stance is neither easy nor comfortable within a traditional academic setting.

There is a very legitimate fear on the part of academic personnel and budget committees that expanding traditional tenure criteria could result in the college awarding tenure to professors with poor publication records, whose understanding of theory is weak, and who once tenured, will have no incentive to continue to produce viable work. To counter that concern, SPA has placed a great deal of emphasis on developing collaborative working relationships that energize and motivate faculty rather than causing them to become complacent. Ironically it is precisely this proximity to practitioners and the challenge of integrating theory and practice under real conditions provided by the model that excites and sustains faculty commitment to serious work within and across disciplines. It opens up unique opportunities for academic inquiry that would not otherwise be accessible. The challenge is to find projects that can contribute to knowledge at the same time as they are transforming practice. That is the so-called sweet spot for coupling strong research programs with strong pedagogy and community engagement.

At the present time there are no compelling structural incentives inherent in the university to support the school's point of view. SPA administrators must rely on a strategy of "artful persuasion" to successfully escort the junior faculty members they employ through the tenure process. Internally they are betting that the potential to reform the academic promotional system is directly linked to the power and success of the collaborative programs they develop in education and other public sector spheres. As those who are granted tenure through this pathway become more senior, administrators hope they will assert an influence on college policy and the decision-making process. Externally, the City University is particularly vulnerable to the influence of public opinion. SPA is counting on those they are partnered with to trumpet their success, and to advocate for more similar programs at other city colleges, thereby providing an incentive to reform the system as a whole.

Enduring Relationships

The relationship between Baruch College SPA and District Two has endured changes in leadership at both institutions. In fact, the various people in the room when the initial partnership was established no longer hold the same positions they did that day. New leaders have embraced this program and developed it further. Elaine Fink was promoted to superintendent when Alvarado took a position in San Diego. Fink continued to develop and strengthen the ALPS program. When Fink decided to become director of the Educational Leadership Academy in San Diego, Shelley Harwayne, renowned author and former principal of the Manhattan New School, assumed the superintendency and is now a regional superintendent. She too places considerable emphasis on leadership development, reviewing curricular materials, and nurturing the relationship with Baruch College SPA. Program coordination at District Two also changed hands, from Tanya Kaufman (still known to many as "the mother of ALPS"), who became a deputy superintendent and is now a local instructional supervisor to Fay Pallen, an expert practitioner with various district-based leadership responsibilities. Similarly, when the presidency of Baruch College and the deanship of the SPA changed hands, the new leadership committed to the relationship wholeheartedly.

The program has also been enriched through the participation of other district partners attracted to our methods through their relationship and compatibility with District Two approaches. Districts Three, Six, and Fifteen shared District Two's approach to literacy instruction, and they provided principals with a similar level of autonomy over budget and personnel decisions. At the same time, the Alternative Schools District was looking for a responsive university partner, and it joined the group as well. The compatibility in approach and need for responsiveness to immediate instructional concerns rendered the ALPS training model relevant and appropriate for aspiring principals in all these districts.

LESSONS LEARNED: WHAT TO LOOK FOR WHEN YOU ARE SEEKING A PARTNER

First, the disclaimer: we should probably state up front that this is not intended to be a definitive list. Rather, it represents our best thinking, based upon the experiences already described. Our thinking is evolving, as will the attributes we look for in our partners, no doubt. We offer it only as a place to begin the search.

Districts Looking for Universities

Lesson 1: Know thyself. Know how you believe students and adults learn; what experiences and support you believe learners need in order to learn best; and what is and is not negotiable.

Lesson 2: Look for a partner who sees "the problem" the way you do—as the need to develop human capital in order to address specific organizational needs within a specific organizational climate.

Lesson 3: Make sure that there is compatibility and agreement at both the administrative and faculty levels.

Lesson 4: Look for partners who respect the complexity of practice and the expertise of practitioners, and who understand both the value as well as the limitations of theoretical knowledge.

Lesson 5: Look for signs of flexibility in the university's past history.

Lesson 6: Look for signs that the faculty is interested in or, even better has had experience in, collaborative work.

Universities Looking for Districts

Lesson 1: Know thyself. Know how you believe students and adults learn, what experiences and support you believe learners need in order to learn best, and what is and is not negotiable.

Lesson 2: Look for partners who respect and value theoretical knowledge and understand the contribution that knowledge can make to practice.

Lesson 3: Look for partners who are willing to devote the people/time it takes for collaborative work to be effective. This may be part of your full-time job, but your partners are likely to have full-time jobs in their districts in addition to the work they do with you.

Lesson 4: Look for partners who are willing to assign the best and the brightest to co-construct and co-teach in the program.

Lesson 5: Look for partners who are willing to identify and recruit aspiring leaders for the program that they later expect to be able to hire as principals.

Lesson 6: Look for partners who are willing to give you access to schools so that aspiring leaders can observe leaders practicing their craft.

Seeking Additional District Partners

Lesson 1: Look for partners whose culture of instruction is similar, and who share your beliefs about how students learn, and the role of the teacher in the learning process.

Lesson 2: Look for partners whose administrative orientation is similar to yours, and who grant a similar level of autonomy to supervisory staff.

Chapter Three

TERMS OF AGREEMENT

Once the partnership was established, the partners faced a range of administrative and programmatic issues. This section is intended to give the reader the substance of what the partners agreed upon and a sense of the issues they struggled with (and, in some cases, continue to struggle with) in order to reach a workable resolution.

ADMISSIONS

Agreement: **Students should move through the program as a cohort.**

Organizing ALPS using a cohort model was a pragmatic response to the fact that admission to the program was limited to the participating districts. Although courses for ALPS would maintain the same "official" names as those for the "regular" program run by the college, their content and pedagogy were expected to differ significantly. In addition, both partners wanted aspiring leaders to see the program as a coherent whole, rather than as a loosely aligned series of discrete classes. They also wanted to shape the curriculum around a scope and sequence of activities and experiences that built upon one another. In order for this plan to work, aspiring leaders had to be able to move through the whole program as an intact unit.

In addition, the partners wanted to organize learning around authentic problems, conditions, and events that novice principals were likely to encounter on the job. In order to work on some of these problems, they wanted to break aspiring leaders into cooperative learning groups and hold the groups responsible for collaboratively developed responses to the assigned challenges. They considered the ability to work in a group a core leadership skill to be mastered. The cohort model provided increased opportunities for instructors to get to know the aspiring leaders as learners and to observe how they worked in a team. These insights informed the composition of the working groups, and they also helped instructors to identify issues and to provide coaching where needed.

A fundamental advantage of the cohort model was its extension beyond the scope of the program. The relationships formed through engagement in intense, collaborative problem solving over time provided graduates with a ready-made professional community to call upon for support as cohort members assumed leadership positions in schools.

Agreement: **In order to be accepted into the program, aspiring leaders must have the approval of both the district and the college.**

Both partners had a stake in the admissions process, but they represented different interests and therefore wanted the process to capture and/or filter out different factors. Traditionally, the university used admissions criteria to determine whether or not an applicant had the intellectual skills to complete the course work successfully. They used past academic record as a predictor of future academic performance, and they used a required essay to evaluate the quality of the applicant's writing. For them, good writing skills were critical to academic success, an indication that the applicant could evaluate the information presented, think about and make sense of complex concepts, develop a cogent argument, and communicate ideas clearly.

The district, however, was primarily interested in whether or not the applicant would make a good principal. For them, past academic success did not represent a reliable means of predicting future leadership performance. Instead, they relied on past job performance to predict future job performance. Furthermore, the writing that most principals had to do (their observations about teachers, letters to teachers and parents, memos to the district office, and the development of plans) did not resemble the admissions essay format at all. Most often, when principals are called upon to communicate their ideas or their vision, it is through a verbal venue (at a meeting of the parent-teacher association [PTA], a staff conference or a meeting with the superintendent or school board). The thinking and communication skills that such occasions required were more relational than written. They were more a matter of the power of persuasion—less about the ability to ponder and write, and more about the ability to think on one's feet.

What emerged was a two-tiered approach to the admissions process. Districts recruited aspiring leaders from among their teachers through a formal posting process.

To be considered, applicants must:

- have taught for a minimum of three years
- be recognized as a master teacher
- hold a master's degree or be willing to work toward one (as it is required for certification)
- have participated in the district's professional development activities
- have excellent oral and written communications skills
- have excellent interpersonal skills
- want to be a principal or assistant principal in the district

To apply, candidates must submit to the district office:

- a completed Baruch College School of Public Affairs application
- a copy of all college transcripts, including evidence of a master's degree or the intent to pursue one
- a resume
- an essay that includes:
  - why they aspire to become a school leader
  - examples of their teaching accomplishments
  - how they see themselves as "change agents" in a school
- and two recommendations, one of which must be from the principal of the applicant's school

Representatives from the district administration then interview candidates. They ask them questions such as:

- What experience have you had as a leader?
- As a school leader you will have to handle difficult situations that involve relationship skills. Tell us about a difficult situation you have had to face in your present position. How did you manage it? How did it turn out?
- What do you think you can bring to the program?

If the panel is concerned that a candidate does not have sufficient curriculum experience, panel members might also ask the candidate to describe the district's approach to a particular content area, and how that approach is being implemented in the candidate's school or classroom. Or, they might visit the applicant's school to conduct an observation and/or have a conversation with the principal.

Once accepted into the program the district is prepared to make a substantial investment in the participant. The district therefore wants to be sure that potential candidates are aware of the commitment they are expected to make in return for this investment. Aspiring leaders typically maintain full teaching loads while they attend the program. As a result of past complaints about competing demands on time and conflicting priorities, the panel prepares applicants for what they can expect by letting them know that the program is extremely rigorous, and the work quite time-consuming. In fact, during the interview process, candidates are asked how they plan to make room in their schedules for all the out-of-class work. In addition, applicants are informed that, if accepted, they will be required to sign a contract expressing a committment to work in the district once the program is completed (described later).

Screened applications are then passed along to the college admissions committee for approval through the regular admissions procedure. The sequencing of the process is important. Pre-screening by the district acts to filter out candidates who might be able to perform well academically but whom the district would not be willing to appoint as principals or assistant principals to lead instruction in their schools.

Agreement: **Candidates who are accepted into the program must sign a contract agreement with the district.**

The district was prepared to bear all or part of the cost of the program to the best of its ability (see Financial Agreement section). In return for this investment, participants are expected to sign a contract with the district stipulating that they will:

- regularly attend and complete course requirements
- remain in the district upon completion of the program for a period of time (generally between three and four years)
- apply in good faith for every vacancy for the position of assistant principal or principal
- if selected by the superintendent for a position, have the right to reject no more than one assignment during the three- or four-year commitment period
- be obligated to repay tuition costs if they default on any of the above contractual agreements

The district arrived at this reciprocal commitment arrangement after several aspiring leaders in the first cohort, in whom they had invested time and money, left the district for positions elsewhere. The strategy mimicked the two-way accountability system the district employed as part of their approach to districtwide professional development at all levels of the organization. The aspiring leader accountability agreement thereby served the district's interest in maintaining a pool of qualified candidates to fill school leadership vacancies, while reinforcing its cultural norms.

TEACHING

Agreement: **Courses will be co-taught by a professor and a practitioner from the participating districts.**

To ensure that the program's curriculum and pedagogy reflected district-held values and belief systems, the district partners wanted to participate actively in the instruction of the courses. To staff the program initially, they recruited and selected principals who espoused those values and beliefs and whom they trusted to model the behaviors and habits of minds they wanted aspiring leaders to acquire. Although, theoretically, the practitioner/instructors could have been enlisted from any of the participating districts, with few exceptions, they came from District Two. As the program matured, however, an alternative source of staffing emerged. Graduates of the program returned to teach in it, giving the instruction an added dimension. Not only did these novice principals believe in the program's guiding principles, they could contribute valuable information about what it was like to practice them as a new principal, or assistant principal, of a real school.

To conform to the university's human resource structures, practitioners working in the program were formally hired as adjuncts by the college. In addition to their regular salary paid by the districts, they received compensation from the college for each course they co-taught at the regular (and meager) adjunct rate. The expense of the co-teaching model was then passed along to the district through the tuition cost structure (see Financial Model section).

The university devoted full-time faculty resources to the program. This was particularly important during the initial stages of development because it helped to ensure enough internal integrity so that the program felt to students like a coherent program rather than a series of discrete courses loosely strung together. As it turned out, the investment had an added advantage. Once the program was up and running, the college was in a position to use what participating faculty had learned to develop an open admissions cohort program based upon the ALPS model. While the open admissions program could not afford many of the accoutrements of ALPS, including the luxury of co-teaching and school site visits, it utilized the same curriculum and reflected the same guiding principles and pedagogy. And, it is fast gaining a reputation for the same high quality.

The college was concerned that program quality for both ALPS and the open admissions program might be compromised in the event of faculty turnover over time. So, they applied for and received a grant from the Stupski Foundation to compile detailed documentation for each course offering. The document was to act as a curriculum guide to orient new faculty to the program. However, while the written records were certainly helpful, the program pedagogy is sufficiently unfamiliar to most professors and practitioner/instructors that the college has found it necessary to consider additional ways to scaffold the learning of new faculty. One method currently in use is to have new faculty members co-teach for a semester with experienced faculty. Other forms of faculty training continue to be explored.

Agreement: **Don't force the model beyond its capacity to do the work.**

The partners did not want adherence to the model to take priority over the goals they had set for the program. Although the ALPS model calls for each course to be co-taught by a professor and a practitioner, some courses in the program do not conform to that ideal. Since none of the college's full-time faculty members were knowledgeable enough about K–12 curriculum issues to be able to make a meaningful contribution to the "Curriculum" course, it has typically been co-taught by practitioner/instructors from the participating districts. The "Law" course is another exception. It has typically been taught by a solo practitioner/instructor who was recruited from the New York City school system, but was not always employed by any of the participating districts.

Agreement: **It's all about relationships.**

Unless you have had one of those rare love-at-first-sight experiences, the dynamics of co-teaching are enigmatic at best. On balance, those in the program who have engaged in it have concluded that it is worth the trouble of working through the difficult spots. Although we have all worked at working out the dynamics, each pair has arrived at a different solution. So, the first lesson to be learned is that there is no right way to do this.

We did, however, notice a pattern in the issues that pairs typically struggled with; among them, was an initial feeling of intimidation. Practitioners reported feeling intimidated by what the professors "knew," because of their status in the community and in the university environment. Professors also reported feeling intimidated by what the practitioners "knew," the tacit knowledge and skill that came from hands-on experience in schools. Some pairs discussed their emotions openly; others did not. All of them reported that their feelings of insecurity began to evaporate as soon as they individually began to find their way into the work of co-construction and co-instruction through their own area of expertise.

Another source of tension was the distribution of the work. For the professors, teaching and research are part of their full-time job. For the practitioner, this work was in addition to their existing full-time jobs. This difference affected the time each had available for activities like planning, assessing student work, and administrative tasks. Again, each pair struggled with the issue in its own way, and each eventually arrived at a balance of shared labor that worked for them.

Among the unanticipated relationship issues, were those involving interactions between the program faculty and the aspiring leaders themselves. Students were profoundly aware that some of their instructors came from the same districts in which they were employed as teachers. This arrangement substantially raised the stakes for them as students, causing some concern about how their classroom performance might affect their chances of becoming principals and assistant principals in those same districts. In fact, this awareness sometimes played itself out in the form of reluctance to engage with full honesty in classroom dialogue about sensitive issues. For these students, having the option to discuss course content with a professor, rather than the practitioner/instructor, provided an opportunity to pursue their learning on more neutral ground.

COURSE CONTENT

Agreement: **The curriculum should be organized around the question, what do principals need know, and be able to do, in order to improve instruction in their schools?**

The decision to make what principals actually needed to know and be able to do the determining factor in what would or would not be included in the program curriculum may seem obvious. However, when the partners examined the existing course outlines in use by the college they found that there was tremendous variability in the relevance of course content to the tasks principals were expected to perform on the job.

The "School Finance" course, for example, had traditionally been organized around the history of, and motivation behind, federal, state, and local fiscal structures. It needed to be almost entirely recast to reflect the information and skills New York City principals needed to master in order to develop budgets designed to support their instructional programs. On the other hand, the course titled "Administration of the Urban School," which already used a problem-based format based on the work of Bridges and Hallinger, required only minor adjustments to conform to the criteria.

Together, program faculty discerned the actual work of principals in the districts where program graduates served. As professors and practitioners worked together to define course content, scope and sequence, each couple struggled in its own way with the tension between the theoretical and the practical, the historical and the contemporary, the big picture and the details of the day-to-day life of principals. The discussion about what to teach forced practitioners and professors alike to explain their thinking to one another, making explicit what had formerly been tacit assumptions about what constitutes useful knowledge. It exposed those assumptions to professional discourse, and these conversations were sometimes difficult. The need to maintain an open mind, and a stance of curiosity and respect for the other's point of view, frequently required professors and practitioners alike to challenge their deeply held beliefs about what matters, and why. Often, the choreography of coming to a workable balance involved a dance that consisted of two steps forward and one step back. Staying with the process, however, served to make transparent and concrete the model of reflective practice that instructors expected aspiring leaders to develop throughout the program.

What continues to emerge out of a continuous engagement in the process are a set of competencies that describe what good leaders know and can do, ideas around which the program continually organizes and reorganizes itself (see the Resources section of this book).

As they identified the content of the work of the principal, instructors also had to discern which activities should be simulated, explored, reflected upon, and practiced during a preservice program. It is, of course, not possible to prepare future school leaders for every foreseeable activity, task, or challenge. Instructors had to prioritize the most important, relevant, and transferable aspects of the principalship and design learning opportunities so that aspiring principals could practice and master them. These activities allowed future principals to see and feel themselves to be school leaders, and helped them make the transition from teacher to principal. In order to make that transition, future leaders needed to be able to think and act their way through the daily demands that most principals face. The most effective learning activities simulated and engaged students in the real work of leading a school using problem-based learning (Bridges and Hallinger 1995).

Through problem-based learning, activities and assignments correspond to authentic activities of most principals. The stakes in these activities are high. Participants are aware that if they do not practice doing these activities during their preservice training, they will ultimately have to perform them for the first time on the job.

Agreement: **The program should feel unified to students, the discrete courses linked.**

Both partners wanted to ensure that the aspiring leaders were exposed to learning experiences that built upon one another. To be able to cross-reference each other's work, each instructor needed to be familiar with the syllabi for the entire program. This approach necessitated joint curriculum planning sessions, in addition to the ones held by each pair to develop individual course content.

As a result of the cross-program planning meetings, there has been an attempt to integrate the work of concurrent courses. For example, in the "Instructional Leadership in Educational Organizations" and "School Finance" courses, what began with the development of a joint final project evolved each year into an increasingly integrated approach to the curriculum. It more authentically mimics the actual work principals are expected to do, in the sequence in which they are expected to do it.

Agreement: **Content deemed essential to principal knowledge and skill that does not fit neatly into any course syllabus should be covered in mini-courses during intersession.**

Some content simply did not fit into the natural logic of the course progression. Rather than compromise that logic, the partners chose to address technical competencies, like the new special education policies and complex human resource issues, through one-day, intensive mini-courses scheduled during the university's intersession. Principals or district office staff members from participating districts typically teach these units of study.

Agreement: **The curriculum should be organized around both fictive and real schools.**

In order to keep the curriculum oriented toward the real work of the principalship, and grounded in a problem-based pedagogic approach, the work is typically focused on problem scenarios and simulations that are based in complex profiles of fictive or real schools. Aspiring leaders work initially with fictive scenarios, and progress to working on real schools in the participating districts.

Constructing a curriculum around real schools is challenging. First, there is the issue of selection. Aspiring leaders make site visits to schools that are later studied in-depth in their "Instructional Leadership" and "School Finance" courses. The partners wanted students to be exposed to, and able to learn from, a wide range of good principal practice at each instructional level—elementary, middle, and high school. However, while successful leaders can provide important insight into how to leverage instructional improvement (what to look for, how to interpret information, what choices to make, and what responses to anticipate), successful schools do not necessarily provide the richest learning experience in which to master those skills. Partners found that sometimes the best learning environments were those in which the building principal was still struggling to orient the school organization toward a clear instructional focus, rather than refining an existing one. Program faculty had to strike a balance between their competing pedagogical interests—models of best practice and complex and challenging learning opportunities.

Second, there is the issue of access. Here the university/district connection proved to be invaluable. District partners had a vested interest in making schools accessible for study. However, depending upon the internal politics of the school and/or district, the selected

principals felt more or less vulnerable to close examination by outsiders. Since their willingness to be investigated is a determining factor in the selection process, the partners discovered the importance
of assessing that willingness up front and, if possible, independent
of any pressure the district might assert. Principals whose schools are
being considered for study need to be made fully aware of what their
participation involves: a teacher culture survey; structured interviews with staff (and, if possible, parents) on-site; daylong visits of
classrooms by approximately twenty-five aspiring leaders, and two
or three instructors; and detailed data analysis. One way to elicit
cooperation from host principals is to invite students to focus their
work around an issue that the principal has identified as a core
school challenge. In this approach, aspiring leaders work as a team
of consultants to the principal. When this model is working well, it
can stimulate a rich exchange between the principal and the aspiring leaders that exposes previously hidden obstacles to successful
implementation of proposed strategies.

Agreement: **Assignments should be designed to provide aspiring
leaders with the opportunity to practice authentic principal leadership activities.**

In order to create assignments that supported the program's curriculum and pedagogy, the partners struggled with the tension between:
the need for graduate-level academic rigor, and the desire for exercises that reflected the real work of principals; the need to assess
individual learning, and the desire to provide opportunities to practice the skills required for group learning.

Conversations about assignment development were most productive when they were focused on defining the competencies that
instructors wanted aspiring leaders to acquire and practice; and
then mapping back from those competencies to create designs for
appropriate learning activities. For example, rather than having students write academic essays to illustrate their facility for astute
observation, rigorous analysis, and cogent argumentation, program
instructors found that these skills could just as easily be demonstrated through authentic tasks. They had them write letters to
school staff or parents, give public presentations of school improvement plans and budgets, write observations of teacher practice, and

write grant proposals. Intrinsic to these tasks are activities that require the development of both individual and collaborative competence.

Agreement: **Readings should be directly linked to practice.**

The program's practice-based, learning-by-doing orientation brought close scrutiny of the assigned readings. These conversations were of two kinds, how much reading should be required, and what should the required reading consist of?

The districts were concerned that aspiring leaders, who already strained under the burden of full-time jobs in addition to their participation in the program, not be further loaded down with heavy reading requirements that did not directly improve their leadership capacities. They also wanted to ensure that the required readings were relevant to the practice of the principalship and reflective of the district's approach to instruction and leadership. Their bias was toward source documents, such as the teacher contract and professional literature, some of which were already in use in district-run, inservice teacher and leadership professional development programs.

For the university, the issue uncovered latent discomfort with the idea of using experiential learning as the primary approach to knowledge acquisition. They were concerned that academic rigor, traditionally dependent upon scholarly reading and writing, might be severely compromised.

The most productive discussions focused on the value-added of the reading material. What did it contribute to student understanding? Was that contribution essential for principal leadership practice? Was that contribution unique, or did students have access to the information through some other program pathway? There are, of course, vast amounts of powerful literature that we believe could enhance a leader's effectiveness; with limited time and multiple demands we used a set of standards to help us select and prioritize the readings in the service of instructional leadership development.

First, course resources must be related to the issues that future leaders are asked to address. Second, they must challenge future leaders to think through complex problems in complex ways (i.e., they should not provide "silver bullet" solutions, checklists, or blueprints for reform). Third, the language must be accessible to practitioners;

and, fourth, they must be orientated toward improved practice, rather than the mere diagnosis or autopsy of bad practice.

There are various useful resources beyond published research, including Internet websites, clearinghouses, and coalitions focused on various facets of school improvement that can connect future principals to professional networks. More importantly, expert practitioners who have successfully met the challenges that future leaders will face can provide the most useful insight, understanding, and feedback to program participants as they work through course assignments. By positing the idea that working principals can serve as resources, preparatory programs reinforce the notion that knowledge is continually co-constructed among people facing similar challenges.

Agreement: **Assessment of student work should model the practices of: having clear expectations, giving extensive feedback, and providing opportunities for revision. Authentic audiences should evaluate project presentations.**

As instructors, we could easily agree that one of the most effective ways of teaching is through modeling what we consider to be best educational practice in our own instructional behaviors. Through the use of rubrics for each assignment we modeled clear expectations and commitment to credible and consistent performance. By making the logic of our course design transparent, we modeled the facilitation of adult learning through collective problem solving and collective knowledge construction. Through our written feedback to program participants, we modeled individualized communication and support. Through program participants' feedback to us, we held ourselves accountable to the aspiring leaders, the districts in which they will work, and each other.

Tension emerged, however, around the issue of grading. Although the participating districts had extensive experience in designing and conducting professional learning experiences, they had done so within the context of a reciprocal accountability system (in which the quality of the adult learning was believed to be highly dependent upon the quality of the teaching and support). The espoused objective of practitioner/instructors was for all aspiring leaders to master the course content and competencies. If students did not meet program expectations practitioners were predisposed to believe that it was largely a reflection of the quality, or design, of their instruction. They were inclined to look inward, and to make the necessary adjustments to their teaching methods. They also expressed concern that grading adults who were selected carefully by the districts and were motivated to achieve high levels of performance was inappropriate. They believed that pass/fail criteria would allow individuals whom the district thought they had selected in error to be counseled to leave the program, and that everybody else should pass.

To put it simply, the university required grades; so, each teaching pair had to work out a balance between that requirement and the process by which they worked to improve their practice.

In addition to feedback and quality assessment by instructors, project-based products are now presented to authentic audiences. These presentation and feedback sessions provide valuable information to both aspiring leaders and instructors on the quality and relevance of their work.

HOW WE TEACH

Our pedagogical approach is grounded in a series of agreements about adult learning in a specific sector and for a specific purpose. These agreements shape not only what we teach, but how we teach. The program provides opportunities to work with real school problems, real school data, and real school budgets. We take our cohorts to site visits of real schools. We hold ourselves accountable for providing our aspiring leaders with opportunities to think like principals, strategize like principals, and act like principals. Our pedagogical approach, therefore, aims to simulate the world of the principal within the confines of the university setting.

Agreement: Adults learn through doing.

Theories of adult learning suggest that adults best internalize new knowledge through experience. Teaching, then, becomes the thoughtful design of learning opportunities that illustrate how to do the work of the principal; how to work through the day-to-day challenges of school leadership; and how to maintain one's focus on instructional effectiveness. Course professors craft simulations, problem scenarios, and analytical approaches to real schools that involve students in the doing of the principalship.

One clear example of the doing in ALPS is the "in-basket" exercise, conducted early in the curriculum. This exercise adapted from the work of Bridges and Hallinger (1995), requires students to confront a series of pressing demands typically found in any given school day, make decisions about how to handle each demand, and evaluate their decision making against the instructional imperative. During this simulation, aspiring leaders observe a teacher (via video-tape) delivering a weak, and even offensive lesson to a group of students that grows increasingly rowdy as the class progresses. They meet with angry parents (role-played by volunteers) who complain about everything, from their son not being challenged enough by the math curriculum, to their daughter being sexually harassed by a fellow student, or a teacher who used a racial slur while talking to their child. Through this experience, aspiring leaders learn how best to manage their time, how to anticipate the consequences of their decisions, and how to focus all of their energies toward their instructional purposes. The work of teaching, in this context, becomes the design of the exercises, simulations, and problem scenarios, along with the careful observation of students' practice, and guided reflection on their approaches.

Agreement: **Adults learn through reflection.**

In addition to experiencing the actual work of the jobs they are training for, adults also learn by reflecting on their decisions, and using that reflection to further their development. Rather than simply experiencing the work of the principal, we ask program participants to reflect on the decisions that they make while performing job-embedded tasks. In that way, they can determine why they make the decisions that they do. Teaching then becomes a matter of posing provocative questions that orient participants' thinking around issues of instruction, equity, and personal and professional assumptions, philosophies, biases and growth, and examine how these play a role in instructional improvement efforts. Guided by a series of questions determined by the instructors through observing student work, the aspiring leaders jointly examine their decision-making strategies, their ways of collaborating, their sense of competence, and their needs as emerging leaders. Reflection is both an individual and a collective endeavor that happens both privately and through conversation.

For example, rather than having open-ended conversations about race and racism, we pose questions about how principals might lead a conversation about student performance assessment data that, when disaggregated by race, reveal racially identifiable achievement patterns. First we give future principals the opportunity to develop strategies and vocabularies for addressing these issues. Then we collectively reflect on those strategies and vocabularies, pushing all program participants and faculty to find the language and behaviors that propel forward an agenda grounded in instructional improvement. Program participants are asked to look closely at themselves and at one another as we sustain difficult, uncomfortable conversations about key features of educational leadership in the context in which they will be working. These complex conversations are integrated into the problem scenarios that guide the preparatory program.

When students are asked to work in groups, time is set aside to discuss their working relationships, the development of group process, and how their experiences here might shape their future work on leadership teams and in collaboration with others. Future leaders are asked to constantly observe themselves as they interact with their colleagues, to try to develop a sense of who they are as leaders, where they feel comfort and discomfort, where they jump in and where they sit back, where their strengths and weaknesses lie. They are asked to remain cognizant of what they are doing and how they are doing it, so that a reflective process becomes second nature.

It is important to engage program participants in reflective conversations with the broader educational community. Members of the school community are invited to serve as audience members for oral presentations. By the time a future leader finishes the program, she or he has made at least three formal presentations to—and received vital feedback from—audiences consisting of working superintendents, deputy superintendents, parents, students, policy officers, foundation program officers, and principals. This process engages program participants in the real work of presenting an improvement strategy to a school's stakeholders while culling the collective knowledge of the community in order to solve a common problem. It gives them the opportunity to practice thinking on their feet as they respond to the questions posed by a diverse, authentic audience.

In addition to facilitating conversations between aspiring leaders and school community members, the role of the instructor is to provide highly individualized feedback on assignments. This activity is a way to engage in direct conversation with individual program participants. The feedback is expected to be thorough, thoughtful, and rigorous. Typically, it takes the form of questions in response to the completed assignments and presentations. For example, if an aspiring leader submits a letter to the school community that uses pedantic language or obscure references, we might ask her or him to reread the letter as a teacher, and then as a parent, to direct attention to the issues of tone and audience (gearing one's message to the intended group of people). If a program participant has difficulty expressing him or herself in writing, we meet with that individual to discuss writing strategies, providing some coaching and suggestions about where to get additional support.

Agreement: **Adults learn through collaboration.**

In order to elicit conversations that will move aspiring leaders forward in their development of skills and content knowledge, the courses place students in purposefully designed working groups for various job-embedded projects. Guided by a specific goal, task, or project, the students work together through conversation and collaboration. Having "thought-partners" for the multiple, daunting tasks of running a school increases the collective knowledge of the individuals in the program and the system as a whole. Group members share their knowledge, the practices of the schools in which they work, their best thinking on how to address a situation, and their wealth of knowledge derived from professional literature. Teaching in this context is a matter of guiding the conversations by selecting the assignments that will elicit the most rigorous and relevant learning, and choosing the most compelling resources (such as research literature, theoretical approaches, and exemplary practice) to guide the aspiring leaders' thinking.

Program instructors also maximize the participants' learning potential through crafting the groups carefully. We start the program with a focus on maximizing the diversity in each learning group (based on every dimension in which diversity might occur, but focusing most prominently on professional experience and school level); when as we get to know the students better, we adjust the composition of learning groups to fit the desired learning. At times, students may select to work alone; but, by the time that decision is an option, most choose to work with others. By the end of the program, we often place certain individuals together because we know that they need to learn specific content or skills from one another.

Agreement: **Adults learn through observation of expert practice.**

There are limitations as to what can be accomplished in the confines of a university classroom. Our program therefore takes aspiring leaders into actual schools, where they can observe master practitioners leading instructional improvement. During these site visits, students speak with the school principals, observe teachers, review plans, and learn how various schools work through the improvement process.

The teaching, then, relies on careful selection of schools, and school leaders, to bring to life strategic points necessary for effective school leadership. As instructors, we focus on a range of schools, at different points in their improvement process. We do not focus only on schools which have consistently high performance. Instead, we focus on schools in which instructional improvement is taking place; on schools in which leaders have altered the school culture through strong, effective instructional practice; and on schools in which specific innovations (such as inclusion approaches to special education, effective ways of developing literacy skills in the upper grades, and working with mostly brand-new teachers) are worthy of dissemination.

The teaching also relies on structuring the school visits so that aspiring leaders walk away with lessons for school leadership. We want to make sure that they leave the school visits with a sense of the real work of the improvement process so that they can use what they have seen. Again, we engage them in reflective conversations that tease out the lessons that can be put into use in new contexts.

Agreement: **Adults learn through thoughtful, written, individualized feedback.**

One of the key roles of program faculty is to provide considerable individual feedback to each program participant. We therefore require both group and individual written projects, and we provide detailed assessments of the students' written work. We engage both the content and form of students' work through written feedback that highlights the strengths of the student submissions, on both substantive and stylistic dimensions, as well as the areas in need of growth. Through this detailed written feedback, the students derive a great deal of understanding about where their strengths and weaknesses lie.

Agreement: **Adults learn through practice.**

Finally, we provide our students with opportunities to actually practice the work of being the principal through summer school internships. Because we have been unable to fund our students' internships during the school year (and they all need to earn a salary while participating in this program), we have devised a summer school internship program in which the district assigns aspiring leaders to run summer schools under the direction of working principals. During these internships, aspiring leaders practice the work of supervising instruction, ordering materials, and building relationships with parents, all in the service of effective teaching and powerful learning for children. Program faculty members supervise the internships, and a weekly seminar frames the experience, allowing participants to come together to work through difficult challenges.

FINANCIAL MODEL

The program's accountability system is based upon a three-way, reciprocal agreement between the aspiring leaders participating in the program, the district that employs them, and the college. This agreement can be described briefly as follows:

Agreement: **The financial structure and the accountability model should be interrelated.**

In exchange for a financial and human capital investment in their principal preparatory education, inservice support and professional development, aspiring leaders agree to: complete all preparatory program requirements; apply for and accept district administrative/supervisory positions; and serve in the district for a specific period of time—usually between three and four years.

In exchange for a financial and human capital investment by the district, as well as access to schools for site visits, the college agrees to: accept into the program only those candidates who meet both district and university requirements; customize program curriculum and pedagogy to reflect district approaches to instruction; and measure program success by on-the-job performance, rather than course completion.

In addition, the districts agree to supply information to the college about aspiring leaders' postgraduation, on-the-job performance creating a feedback loop that makes possible a cycle of continuous program improvement.

Central to this accountability structure is the ability of the district to invest in the aspiring leader's preparatory education. Most districts assume the full cost of tuition, as well as associated expenditures, for their aspiring leaders; one of the partners shares the tuition costs fifty-fifty with students.

The financial structure employed to determine the cost of tuition for a single cohort of twenty-five aspiring leaders may be expressed as shown in Figure 3–1.

The cost of tuition, however, does not represent the whole cost of the program to participating districts. In addition to tuition, there is a set of associated hidden, or unrealized, costs assumed by the district as part of their investment in the program. These include:

- Program coordination
- Planning time
- Release time for aspiring leaders to make site visits to schools

Courses	"Administration of the Urban School"	1 full-time faculty	1 adjunct	books & materials
	"Curriculum"		2 adjuncts	books & materials
	"Law"		1 adjunct	books & materials
	"Urban School Community"	1 full-time faculty	1 adjunct	books & materials
	"Instructional Leadership"	1 full-time faculty	1 adjunct	books & materials
	"Introduction to School Finance"	1 full-time faculty	1 adjunct	books & materials
	Internship semester #1	1 full-time faculty	1 adjunct	books & materials
	Internship semester #2 (summer)		1 adjunct	books & materials
Mini-Courses	Occasional guest presenters			honorarium
	4 per cohort			honorarium
	Food			estimated cost
Administration	Technology Support	10 percent full-time person		
	College Administrative Support	50 percent full-time person		
	Program Director	2/7 faculty time		
	OTPS (other than personal service)			estimated cost

Figure 3–1

We estimate the value of these hidden costs to be about 50 percent of a midrange teacher's salary.

There is no getting around it; this is not an inexpensive model. If we compare tuition for the ALPS program with that of the regular SAS program run by Baruch College School of Public Affairs, tuition for ALPS is approximately twice the cost of the college's regular program. Arguably, the difference is attributable to the value of customization and accountability.

Reducing the number of courses co-taught by full-time faculty could reduce tuition costs substantially, but the college has been reluctant to exercise this option. They believe that to do so would compromise the commitment they have made to the program. From their point of view, direct involvement of full-time faculty is the cornerstone of the synergistic relationship between theory and practice which lies at the heart of the ALPS experiment.

Initially, most districts managed the high cost of tuition (and, presumably, the associated hidden costs as well) through the use of competitive and reimbursable entitlement grants.

In the fall of 2002, as a result of mandated budget cuts and a new collective bargaining agreement with the teachers' union, districts were confronted with a substantial budget reduction. Understandably, they were compelled to focus all of their available resources on maintaining instructional programs, a move that severely compromised principal leadership capacity building efforts. That is, they could no longer bear the burden of providing sole support for the program.

Agreement: **A cost-sharing model to manage hard times.**

By this time, ALPS had such a strong reputation that the cohort enrolling in the program in the fall 2002 semester was reportedly willing to absorb tuition costs. However, without a financial commitment on the part of the districts, superintendents had no way to leverage a professional commitment from aspiring leaders. In addition, from the perspective of the college, if the program were solely financed through student contribution it might severely compromise the district's commitment to a rigorous admissions process and weaken their participation in feedback structures upon which the accountability system relied to determine program success.

Together the partners decided to seek short-term, outside funding to cover a portion of tuition costs for the cohorts already enrolled in the program. It was agreed that if such a funder could be identified, the districts, college, and aspiring leaders would shoulder the remaining portion. That is, a cost-sharing model was developed whereby:

- the college would reduce tuition by 10 percent
- an estimated 50 percent of the adjusted tuition would be funded through private sources
- the district would contribute 25 percent of the adjusted tuition
- and aspiring leaders would contribute the remaining 25 percent of the adjusted tuition.

The request to the funder was for one year only. The idea was to solve the immediate problem and use the time to figure out a more sustainable funding strategy.

What is remarkable, as we move forward, is the strength of the partners to sustain the relationship even in the face of hard fiscal realities.

ADMINISTRIVIA

The administrative difficulties of managing two entrenched bureaucracies while trying to shape, reshape, and teach a complex and rigorous curriculum cannot be overstated.

Agreement: **The program will follow the district's school calendar.**
The districts and the college are organized in accordance with different calendars. The academic semester begins before the district's school year does, and the two institutions have different vacation schedules. In addition, there are some school-based activities, like parent/teacher night, that the district prioritizes over preparatory program class attendance. The partners therefore resolved to follow the district school calendar with allowances made for special events.

This decision had an impact on space arrangements, book ordering, grade submission requirements, faculty vacations, and tuition payment schedules, all of which have had to be worked through but were never completely routinized due to staff turnover.

Agreement: **Administrative tasks will be distributed among the partners along logical lines.**

The partners agreed that the districts would be responsible for those tasks under their authority:

- the logistics of school site visits
- internship support and supervision
- video examples of practice

The college would be responsible for those tasks that fell into its domain:

- orientation for new cohorts
- arrangements for classroom space
- employee payroll management
- student registration for classes
- student immunization records
- instructional materials duplication
- provisional certification procedures for graduating cohorts
- compilation and mailing of materials to the state for SAS certification

For those tasks that bridged the partnership, such as admissions, each partner would attend to those tasks that fell into its realm:

- as required by collective bargaining agreement, the districts would post the ALPS flyer to attract potential candidates, make sure that candidates filled out applications properly, and deliver completed applications to the college;
- the college would process the applications and notify applicants of acceptance to the program and dates of orientation.

Agreement: The "lead" district would assume responsibility for most administrative tasks allocated to the districts, in exchange for a reduction in tuition.

While some administrative tasks were distributed evenly among the partner districts, for example, recruitment and admissions processes, others (such as arranging for school site visits) became the responsibility of the lead district. The partners agreed that in exchange for this work the lead district should be compensated. That compensation came in the form of a reduction in tuition costs for lead district candidates.

FEEDBACK LOOPS AND CONTINUOUS IMPROVEMENT

Agreement: The program should be modeled after a learning organization.

The program faculty, although representing differences of perspectives and preferences on programmatic approaches, was of one mind on the following three beliefs:

- The curriculum is an organic entity that should be responsive to new contextual realities and current best thinking.
- The work should be evaluated regularly by participating students, program graduates, and their employers (district-level leaders).
- The work is collaborative; all courses rely on the thinking of all participating faculty members, irrespective of who is teaching which class.

Agreement: Feedback should be ongoing and multileveled.

In every class, there are numerous opportunities for feedback (through formal and informal written communication, talk-back sheets, mid- and end-of-semester evaluations). For every cohort, an unaffiliated college staff member conducts focus groups of student subgroups to explore their perceptions of program relevance and effectiveness, as well as elements of the program that might be lacking.

Periodic meetings with district-level leaders (superintendents and deputy superintendents) from each district are held to evaluate the program based on the on-the-job performance of graduates. Through these various mechanisms, we determine which elements of the curriculum are strong, which need fine-tuning, and which need substantial revision.

The conversations begin with questions about how the individual courses and overall program prepare aspiring leaders for the work of the principal. We then ask how the courses and program could be altered to better prepare future leaders for this role. We have found that the feedback we receive is rigorous and grounded in the collective goal of developing serious, thoughtful, and effective instructional leaders. Based on that feedback, we have altered the content, scope, and sequence of the curriculum, and we have developed linkages between courses in the program.

In addition, program faculty meet frequently to realign, redesign, and hone program components, based on the feedback they receive from the students, graduates, and their collective experience teaching in the program. Faculty members work collectively and continuously to resolve the problems of scope and sequence, develop appropriate assignments that build on one another throughout the course of study, and tie the work of individual courses to a common understanding of program goals. As a result, the internship experience, sequence of assignments, use of technology, use of school visits throughout the curriculum, and overall program order have all changed over the years that the ALPS has been in operation.

Finally, since we operate within a system with rules that frequently change (new local, state, and federal policies; new curricular approaches; new innovations in instruction; new leadership), the program demands flexibility in content to ensure that our program graduates are prepared for the realities of the system in which they will work. This new information is fed into the program by the partners and adjustments to curriculum are made where appropriate. For example, at this writing, the district boundaries are being redrawn into larger regions, the various leadership positions reconfigured, and the curricula aligned throughout the city. ALPS' next semester courses need to be altered to accommodate these new arrangements.

Even as we maintain a focus on best practice, we have had to be flexible and cognizant of the shifts in the environment that hosts our preparatory program, providing us with the opportunity to make new (rather than the same) mistakes each and every year.

CHAPTER FOUR

CURRICULUM AND RESOURCES

Our work has rendered various products that may be of benefit to school districts and universities seeking to prepare future school leaders in effective and rigorous ways. We have developed course materials, as well as guiding principles, for the work of training instructional leaders. The "Principles for Principals," below, guides our leadership development efforts and is woven into the fabric of what and how we teach.

Principles for Principals

- Leaders lead by explicitly modeling the values and behaviors they want the school community to reflect.

- Leaders attend to the gap between espoused beliefs and actions in practice.

- Leaders understand that people have diverse competencies and distribute responsibility and authority in accordance with that understanding.

- Leaders know that instructional improvement is a matter of adults learning to improve their practice, as evidenced in student work. They organize every aspect of the organization for it, include everyone in it, and ensure that it is focused and purposeful and reflective of shared understandings about how adults learn best.

- Leaders acknowledge the reciprocal relationship between accountability and investment in adult learning.

- Leaders maintain a narrow focus over time.

- Leaders stay focused on their purpose amid the day-to-day distractions.

- Leaders connect the parts through a common framework to ensure a cohesive whole.

- Leaders align each and all organizational structures, processes, decisions, and actions with their purpose.

- Leaders are mindful of constructing a bridge that links past, present, and future.

- Leaders are aware of the larger community context in which the school exists.

- Leaders hold themselves accountable.

ALPS courses now follow a sequence that we altered a couple of times before we were satisfied. We begin with two concurrent courses in the fall semester. The first, "Administration of the Urban School," uses a problem-based learning format and places aspiring leaders in the role of the principal. The second, "Curriculum Development and the Improvement of Instruction," moves participants from thinking about curriculum for a classroom full of students to thinking about curricular approaches and staff development opportunities for an entire school. During the next semester, we focus on a class called "Urban School Community Leadership," on building community within and around a school, and leveraging community support for school-based initiatives. In it, we address issues of race and racism, and class and classism, as they shape the relationships between schools and the communities that they serve. In tandem with this course, we teach a course called "Law" for school administrators. This is one of the weak links in our program; we do not believe that we have yet arrived at the optimal way to teach the information (we will explain our thinking about this course content later). In addition, we conduct internship seminars in which students make school site visits, meet to discuss their school-based internship projects, and to prepare for the work of running a summer school program. During the summer, aspiring leaders are responsible for running a summer school as part of their internship assignment and meet weekly for reflective seminars. Finally, in the subsequent fall semester, students take two interwoven classes, "Instructional Leadership in Educational Organizations," and "Introduction to School Finance." The following sections provide the reader with details about the structure and organization of, as well as the logic behind, those courses. In presenting this material we have retained the divergent voices and styles of the founding instructors.

ADMINISTRATION OF THE URBAN SCHOOL

Purpose
- to introduce aspiring leaders to the role of the principalship as instructional leadership as well as the day-to-day work of the principal
- to develop effective work habits for collaborative decision making, distributed leadership, time management, agenda setting, meeting management, group work, public speaking, and action planning
- to hone written and oral skills for communication with the school community
- to increase content knowledge about vision setting, professional development models, and safety and violence prevention
- To familiarize students with technological communication options, such as email, message board forums, file shares, and PowerPoint presentations

Instructors
This course is co-designed and co-taught by a university professor (ideally, with pedagogical experience and/or training in problem-based learning) and a practitioner (ideally, a working principal or vice principal, at any level, with demonstrated success at school improvement).

Session 1

Learning Goals

During the first session, the instructors deliver a PowerPoint presentation that reviews the main components of the course. Students learn that the course is taught using a problem-based learning approach: they will work on three problem scenarios during the course of the semester. Through problem-based learning, the work of the principal is simulated in a contrived environment. Students are asked to work on real school-based problem scenarios—each of which has been adapted considerably from the original, written by Bridges and Hallinger (1995)—and to come up with an action plan for addressing those scenarios. In each problem scenario, students take on the role of the principal or assistant principal, analyze the key issues of the school, determine what resources are available to them, and strategize how they will turn the school around. Students present their plans for change to a real audience of working principals and district office personnel.

On the first night of class, students learn that they will work in the same learning groups to which they were assigned by the instructors ahead of time (groups of five to seven students are designed so as to maximize the experiential and professional diversity of each group), for the duration of the semester. The instructors review the theory and practice of problem-based learning, as well as the class norms, the syllabus, assignments, and due dates. They also review the cooperative learning group roles that students will use to work on three problem scenarios, a protocol for problem-solving, a model for effective discussion and agenda setting, the "free-rider" problem (group members who are not contributing much to the group), and the online communication technologies that students will use to communicate with one another outside of class. At the end of the first session, students meet in preassigned work groups to determine who will take on which cooperative learning group role (e.g., facilitator, manager, timekeeper, recorder, and group member) for each session of the rest of the semester (students are instructed to rotate the roles so that everyone has a chance to practice every role).

At the end of Case 1, students will submit a letter to the school community, detailing the school's priorities for the upcoming year.

Frame

This session provides the context for the work of the rest of the semester. The instructors set forth the schedule of activities, and lay the expectations for the course. In this session, students realize the rigorous nature of the program, the course, and the work of the principal.

Activities

Review of information by instructors

Participant introductions

Introduction to Case 1

First meeting of working groups

Role assignment within working groups

Session 2

Learning Goals

Students meet in their working groups. Together, they work on the problem scenario entitled "Creating a Vision and the Time to Achieve It" (Bridges and Hallinger 1994) adapted by the instructors to reflect the specific realities of the districts in which the students will work. The persons assigned to be the "managers" of their groups that night come prepared with an agenda for the establishment of a vision statement for the school in Case 1. The agenda should have a meeting goal at the top of the sheet, with a series of activities that lead toward that ultimate goal, and time allotments for each agenda item.

Students work together to determine their vision statement for the Case 1 school, practicing the cooperative learning group roles, and constructing knowledge on school-level analysis for effective leadership.

Frame

Group decision making is challenging, but given a clear agenda, it can move quite rapidly and effectively. The process of collaborating on a vision statement is equally important, if not more important, than the vision statement itself.

Activities

Groups work during the duration of the session to analyze the Case 1 school, using articles that they read for the purposes of this activity. One student in each group sets the agenda for that group's meeting. The agenda typically includes analysis of the case and the creation of a vision statement. After analyzing the case, the groups each come up with a vision statement that is read to the entire group at the end of class. When the energy level seems high and the groups are working on their analysis of the school in the case, the instructors interrupt the class to ask each individual to jot down two to three adjectives that describe how they are feeling about the meeting (on an unsigned piece of paper). While the groups continue to work on their vision statements, the instructors compile these adjectives and write them onto a flip chart. Before the groups present their vision statements to the whole class, the instructors present the list of adjectives (which often include a range of feelings, from inadequacy to hopefulness, and annoyance to competence) to demonstrate the level of contradictory emotions that shape most meetings. The class closes with a discussion of the group processes used to arrive at the vision statements, and the importance of participating in the process.

Debrief

There are many processes for analyzing a school. Attention to strengths and how a leader can build on them is fundamental to asset-based leadership. The combination of pressure and support is crucial, once the leader has determined the appropriate and most effective pressure points and the relevant support structures necessary for instructional improvement.

The review of the various vision statements illustrates how, given the same information, groups can focus on different aspects of a school. We also discuss the importance of participating in the process of setting a vision, and how to maximize the number of participants in that process without losing the effectiveness of the group work.

At the end of this session, the instructors reflect back to the students their observations about the activities that seemed to enhance collaboration, and those that seemed to hinder it. They also discuss strategies for effective group work, such as the establishment of a clear process. One of the class mantras is If you don't have clear process, you rely solely on personality.

Session 3

Learning Goals

To experience the work of the principal through a session-long simulation entitled the "in-basket."

Frame

The work schedule of the principal can be hectic, fragmented, and unpredictable. In order to maximize the time spent on instructional leadership, principals must put into place systems for addressing the daily concerns and issues that are raised. Because a lack of predictability is part of the work, effective leaders must grow comfortable with that atmosphere.

Activities

In the in-basket activity, students are each given a stack of papers with instructions at the beginning of class. They are informed that they are in their third week of the principalship at the school in Case 1, and that they have two hours to address the twenty-five items in the in-basket. The items range from new teachers seeking advice, to parents' groups interested in test score results; and from requests for documents from the district office, to teachers who cannot make it to school that day. Students work through the items in the in-basket individually, indicating how they would handle each situation in writing. During their two hours of work on the various items, they also face two live interruptions. First, the secretary (played by one of the course instructors) informs them (one at a time) that an irate parent is at the school to see them. The secretary escorts the aspiring leader to meet with an actual person who plays the role of the angry parent. Second, a fire alarm is sounded, and the students all have to evacuate the classroom in which they are doing the in-basket activity. Additionally, at a predetermined point in time, the students also conduct an observation of a teacher (via videotape).

At the end of the session, Case 2, "Something Old, Something New, and the Principal's Blues" (Bridges and Hallinger 1995) is distributed.

Debrief

At the end of the session, we discuss the various items of the in-basket that the students found difficult or challenging. We also talk about how one might group the various items so as to create systems to address them in the most efficient and effective way. Students share their strategies for putting into place systems that are consistent with their instructional priorities. We also discuss the importance of distributive leadership and how to develop leadership within the teaching staff. Finally, we answer any questions about district-level support mechanisms for some of the challenging items.

At the end of this session, the instructors review the assignment that is due the following week. Students are to write a letter to the school community that details their priorities for the school in the upcoming year. A rubric for assessing the letters is included in the syllabus.

Session 4

Learning Goals

We start this session with continued discussion of the in-basket activity. Now that students have had some time to digest the exercise, we review ways to group the various items in the in-basket and discuss how to prioritize the systems that need to be put in place. We consider the issue of the ineffective teacher (whose lesson was observed on videotape) and the various options principals have available to them if they need to dismiss an incompetent teacher.

After this discussion, the instructors introduce Case 2, "Something Old, Something New, and the Principal's Blues," also written by Bridges and Hallinger (1995) and adapted by the instructors. The school in Case 2 has both veteran and novice teachers, and the principal needs to devise appropriate professional development opportunities to enhance the learning about instruction of all staff members. The instructors review the readings assigned for this case, with attention to work on professional development, school community building, school organization and culture, adult development and learning theory, and change management. The instructors also review frameworks for analyzing the information on the teaching staff, such as the work of Alan Boyle (2001), from the United Kingdom, on turning around low-performing schools.

For this case, students will need to (a) write a letter to their staff, informing them of the professional development plans for the school, (b) deliver a PowerPoint presentation to the superintendent and her or his cabinet, and (c) submit an action plan to the instructors.

Frame

As instructional leaders, principals have to assume the responsibility of the adult learning among the teaching staff. They have to organize for adult learning about instructional effectiveness. They have to know about how adults learn and they need to schedule the school day so as to maximize the school's capacity to improve instruction.

Activities

Discussion of in-basket exercise

Introduction to Case 2

Work in groups to analyze Case 2 and to divide up resources/readings for case.

Debrief

At the end of this session, the instructors reflect back to students some themes that are emerging in their conversations.

Session 5

Learning Goals

Students will think through the issues of a school in systematic and rigorous ways. Application of the resources and readings supplied with this case allows for grounded analysis of complex problems. Analysis of longitudinal student performance data can frame how a principal might approach teachers at grade level.

Frame

There are many ways to analyze a school's instructional staff. Looking at the information by age, years of teaching experience, capacity (rating through observation), grade level, student performance data, or personality characteristics provide insight in the most effective ways to make use of the current staff and move them to higher levels of instructional performance.

Activities

Instructors lead the students through an analysis of longitudinal student performance data from the school in Case 2. After they have tied the student performance data to teacher profiles, and used the matrix from Boyle (2001) to think about staff needs and assets, students meet in their groups. The manager of each group sets the agenda for how the class time will be used.

Debrief

The instructors reflect back and/or challenge themes and assumptions that they hear from the various groups by posing questions such as, if you had to focus on a specific grade level at the expense of others, which one would it be? or, how does your plan relate to the specific members of your staff? Students do not answer these questions for the whole class, but rather reflect on them in their groups.

Session 6

Learning Goals

Students will learn to use the PowerPoint program.

Students will develop their action plans for the school in Case 2.

Frame

As collective, collaborative analysis and planning grow deeper, solutions emerge.

Activities

The instructors teach the students how to use PowerPoint at a computer lab.

Groups meet to devise strategies and develop an action plan. One group member sets the agenda for the meeting.

Debrief

At the end of the session, the instructors pose questions based on the work of the groups.

Session 7

Learning Goals

Students will develop their action plans for the school in Case 2.

Frame

As collective, collaborative analysis and planning grow deeper, solutions emerge.

Activities

Students work in groups on their action plans.

Debrief

Instructors circulate among the groups, pushing the thinking further by posing questions about the content and processes of students' decisions.

Session 8

Learning Goals

Students will understand the need for carefully articulated plans that are grounded in the reality of their schools. Students will learn how to employ various, plausible strategies at the same school. Students will think on their feet. Students will manage the stress of delivering presentations to adults. Students will learn to focus their reform efforts, to prioritize instruction, to orient any community building within a school around instruction, and to think creatively about solutions to complex problems.

Frame

District personnel and working principals provide useful insight for thinking through complex problems that they themselves have faced. The best expertise on thinking about practice is among practitioners.

Activities

Students deliver PowerPoint presentations in groups, detailing their action plan for the Case 2 school. A panel composed of district personnel and working principals plays the role of the superintendent and his or her cabinet, posing questions, and making comments on the presentations.

Debrief

We review the various presentations; make some general comments on the presentations as a whole; and talk about presentation styles, persuasion, use of evidence, and students' overall plans. At the end of this session, Case 3 is distributed.

Session 9

Learning Goals

Students will analyze their own presentations in lieu of the comments provided by the panel, and make adjustments to their action plans. Students will begin to analyze Case 3. Students will learn to reflect on their group processes.

During this session, students are introduced to Case 3, entitled "Safety and Order" (Bridges [n.d.]) and adapted by the instructors to fit the local context. In this case, students are challenged to address issues of school safety, violence prevention, and some of the ways in which schools perpetuate negative stereotypes of youth.

Frame

Through purposeful reflection on a group process, groups can become more high functioning and efficient in their work.

Activities

Entire class debriefs presentations from prior week.

Students work on action plans.

Instructors introduce Case 3 and accompanying readings.

Instructors meet with each group to review group processes, and goals for the next case.

Debrief

Instructors reflect back common themes from groups as they approach Case 3.

Session 10

Learning Goals

Discipline and violence prevention are highly emotive issues in school leadership. Notions of justice, racism, and differential treatment for similar behaviors emerge in discussions of codes of conduct, rules, regulation, and "punishment." School leaders need to become comfortable with issues of diversity and pluralism as they devise plans for school safety and violence prevention. All of the members of the broader school community need to be involved in crafting plans that are just and fair to all students.

Frame

School structures and curriculum are just as important as, if not more important than, individual student behaviors. School leaders set the tone, shape the structures, and guide the instruction that will support a safe environment for learning.

Activities

Students work in groups on their action plans and PowerPoint presentations. One group member sets the agenda for the group's meetings.

Debrief

The instructors pose questions based on their observations of the group work. When students are not tackling important aspects of the case, the instructors will ask questions about purpose and specific plans to direct some of the thinking.

Session 11

Learning Goals

Students will probe their assumptions and learn to think about schools as a system. They will focus their plans on framing problems as located within schools (rather than within individual children).

Frame

School structures shape student behaviors. Any decisions made about how to address an issue of safety and violence prevention will produce consequences. School leaders need to predict the consequences of any potential decisions they may make.

Activities

Students work in groups to further develop their action plans and PowerPoint presentations. One group member sets the agenda for the group's meetings.

Debrief

The instructors pose questions based on their observations of the group work. When students are not tackling important aspects of the case, the instructors will ask questions about purpose and specific plans to direct some of the thinking.

Session 12

Learning Goals

Students come to agreement about how to address a tricky issue, knowing that the solution will not satisfy all of the stakeholders.

Frame

School leaders cannot satisfy all constituents. Their decisions have to be consistent with their core beliefs, and in the interest of student learning. All school challenges can be framed as instructional issues.

Activities

Students hammer out final problems in their plans and prepare to make their presentations to the school community.

Debrief

Lingering issues and anticipated questions are addressed.

Session 13

Learning Goals

Students will understand the need to make carefully articulated plans that are grounded in the reality of their schools. Students will

PRINCIPAL TRAINING ON THE GROUND

learn various, plausible strategies to use at the same school. Students will learn to think on their feet. Students will manage the stress of making a presentation to adults. Students will learn to focus their reform efforts, to prioritize instruction, to orient any work on safety and violence prevention around instruction, and to think creatively about solutions to complex problems.

Frame

There are many ways to analyze a school-based, violent incident. The way that school personnel define problems has serious implications for any plans they make to address those problems. Assessing an incident from various vantage points and perspectives will lead to more complex and effective solutions.

Activities

PowerPoint presentations and feedback from a panel of district personnel and working principals.

Debrief

We review the various presentations; make some general comments on the presentations as a whole; and talk about students' presentation styles, use of persuasion, use of evidence, and overall plans.

Session 14

Learning Goals

Inventory of the learning the class has done. Focus on group processes, collective decision making, collaboration, leadership, and how to organize schools for instruction.

Frame

Hard work should be celebrated.

Activities

Celebration of semester's work

Reflection on learning, both substantive and process-oriented

Debrief

The work of the principal is often intense, varied, and fragmented; yet the focus on instructional leadership is crucial to school improvement. Students share their experiences of the class, connecting their experiences to their work in schools, the principals with whom they work, and their goals for their own future leadership. The instructors preview the classes that come in the next semester, tying in the themes of this class.

A note on readings: Course instructors should select the most relevant and recent resources to support, guide, and frame their students' learning. The reading resource list should evolve constantly and reflect the current realities of the school leadership. In the past, authors have included:

C. Achilles	S. Lal
R. Ackerman	Lichtenstein et al.
R. Andrea	J. W. Little
R. Andrews	R. Maurer
F. Aquila	G. W. McGiboney
J. Barron	M. McLaughlin
R. Barth	R. Miller
C. Bowditch	P. Morse
A. Boyle	S. N. Oja
M. Bratlien	N. Onishi
D. Clay	K. Peterson
S. R. Covey	D. Prothrow-Stith
T. Deal	M. A. Raywid
G. Donaldson	K. Roane
J. Devine	D. Rohde
R. Evans	J. Scarnati
A. A. Ferguson	T. Sergiovanni
M. Fullan	C. Shields
A. Hargreaves	W. Smith
W. Hawley	L. Stevahn
P. Hodne	L. Valli
M. Ikram	R. Van der Bogert
D. Johnson	L. Walters
R. Johnson	

CURRICULUM DEVELOPMENT AND THE IMPROVEMENT OF INSTRUCTION

Purpose

We designed this course to address the third of our core beliefs:

- You need to know it in order to lead it.

In co-constructing the course, we struggled with the question; what do principals need to know in order to lead curriculum? How much do they need to know about each content area? And, what do they do when they don't know?

The course is set within the context of core beliefs one and two:

- School leadership is focused on instructional improvement. The evidence of school improvement resides in the quality of student work.

- The greatest predictor of student learning is the quality of the teaching, and the most powerful pathway to the improvement of teaching is through adult learning.

Conditions for Effective Learning

We begin with the question—how do people learn best?—because beliefs about how people learn are at the heart of practitioners' choices about what to teach and how to teach it. We encourage aspiring leaders to reflect on who they are as learners, to think about what constitutes a good learning experience, and what sorts of things get in the way of their learning. We urge them to link these shared personal reflections to the research, and co-construct with instructors a set of commonly held *conditions for effective learning*. And then develop "habits of mind and practice" around these conditions, by applying them throughout the program. Within the context of this course, they are asked to think critically about what constitutes effective professional development, and use it as a rubric for evaluating the work of the aspiring leaders' group work.

Readings

In the past, readings have included selections from:

J. D. Bransford, A. L. Brown, and R. R. Cocking, eds. *How People Learn: Brain, Mind, Experience, and School.* (1999)

B. Cambourne. *Conditions for Learning.* (1988)

M. Knowles. "How Adults Learn, Average Rate of Retention." (1970)

L. Resnick and M. W. Hall. *Principles of Learning.* (1998)

Articulating a Philosophy of Education

To explore the implications beliefs about how people learn has on leadership practice, we place the co-constructed Conditions for Effective Learning within a theoretical framework, and demonstrate to aspiring leaders how a coherent philosophy of education helps to guide decisions about curriculum, classroom instruction, what forms of professional development to employ, and how to assess student and adult learning. We also provide aspiring leaders with opportunities to experience how conversations about this topic can help to develop a sense of shared purpose within a school community. In so doing, we have come to believe that for such a philosophy to be useful, it needs to articulate a belief:

- About how people learn
- The role of the teacher in that learning
- The role of the student in that learning
- The type of curricula to be used
- The type of learning activities or teaching strategies to be employed
- The type of materials to be used
- And the types of assessments that best measure student performance

Making the Shift from Teacher to Principal Leader Explicit

The districts reported that novice principals often had difficulty making the shift from being teachers, teaching students, to being principals leading adult learning. To make this transition explicit aspiring leaders are given opportunities throughout the program to practice and internalize making the shift. We found that one of the primary differences in point of view between the two roles, was that while most aspiring leaders espoused the belief that all students can learn, it was hard for many to place faith in the efficacy of the adult equivalent.

Change Theory: If we continue to do what we're doing, we'll continue to get what we're getting.

We are clear up front that improvement means change. To get better at what we do, we need to change the way we do it; or, as Michael Fullan puts it in *Leading in a Culture of Change* (2001) "reculturing is the name of the game." Issues of how to manage the anxiety generated by leading change are woven throughout the program. In this course, we focus attention on two of the most powerful avenues available to a principal leader trying to leverage changes that will result in improved student performance—curriculum and professional learning. We want aspiring leaders to understand that the two are inextricably linked, that there is no knowledge construction or understanding for students (or adults) without something substantive to construct knowledge or understanding around, namely content.

To help cohort members grasp the critical role of professional learning in school improvement, we expose them to the growing body of evidence that teacher knowledge and skill have a profound effect on student performance and that professional learning can positively affect teacher knowledge and skill. We structure opportunities for aspiring leaders to think about how this understanding informs how principals manage curriculum and professional learning in their schools.

Readings

In the past, readings have included selections from:

L. Darling-Hammond. *Why Teaching Matters.* (1997)

R. F. Elmore with D. Burney. *Investing in Teacher Learning: Staff Development and Instructional Improvement in Community School District #2, New York City.* (1997)

M. Fullan. *Leading in a Culture of Change.* (2001)

L. B. Resnick and M. W. Hall. "Learning Organizations for Sustainable Education Reform." (1998)

W. L. Sanders and S. P. Horn. "The Tennessee Value-Added Assessment System (TVAAS): Mixed-Model Methodology in Educational Assessment." (1994)

H. Wenglinsky. "How Teaching Matters." (2000)

Content-Specific Professional Learning

The district partners wanted to be sure that novice principals, entering their schools, had a rudimentary understanding of the theory behind, as well as the components and language of, the curricular approaches or models they had adopted, such as a balanced literacy approach to English language arts. In addition, we wanted to provide aspiring leaders with the experience of a distributive leadership model for professional learning, practice in designing and leading content-specific professional development, and opportunities to assess professional learning experiences in accordance with the conditions of effective learning we had co-constructed.

Ideally, we would have preferred members of the cohort to take responsibility for both the overview learning and the group assignment (see Group Assignment on page 92) during the sessions devoted to content-specific professional learning. As it turned out, that was not practical. So, typically instructors take responsibility for presenting an overview of the topic, and aspiring leaders organize their professional learning experience around a component or part (for example, instructors might give an overview of balanced literacy and one group might focus on the guided reading component of a balanced literacy program). We have found it useful to talk about how to give feedback so that others can hear it at the first session.

When time allows, these sessions can be used to address other topics aspiring leaders are likely to encounter as they lead instructional improvement. For example, how to assess what the staff knows and what they need to learn next, how to manage staff resistance, how to approach veteran teachers, how to support novice teachers and manage tension between belief systems concerning teaching and learning. Often, these topics are clued by what aspiring leaders have observed in their own schools and have shared in discussions with the cohort.

Readings

In the past, readings have been selected by instructors to address the relevant topics.

Materials

- Standards and/or Curriculum Framework K–12 for all content areas
- Information on the district approach to the content area, for example, a description of the components of a balanced literacy program
- Aspiring leader–developed resource lists

Weaving It All Together

Ever since Bryk and others (1993) implanted in our minds the image of schools as Christmas trees with the latest innovations hanging like ornaments next to dated silver bullet programs, and Fullan enjoined us to "Attack . . . overload, fragmentation and incoherence" (Fullan [1997], Lesson 7) it has become increasingly clear that principal leaders need to become "integrators and synthesizers." Aspiring leaders explore the use of approaches like backward planning, curriculum mapping, and curriculum integration to create instructional coherence.

Readings

In the past, readings have included selections from the work of Michael Fullan, Grant Wiggins, and Heidi Hayes Jacobs.

Student Assessment: The Link Between Curriculum, Professional Learning, and Student Achievement

It is important for aspiring leaders to understand the purpose behind curriculum choices—why, when, and how a principal leader introduces new curriculum. To make the connection between curriculum, student learning, and professional learning explicit in their work. We invite them to think about:

- How to evaluate student work and use it as the basis for improving instruction. How to create an environment in which teachers look critically at the curriculum, identifying its strengths and gaps—which students it worked for and which students it does not. This work often provides an opportunity for instructors to challenge some the aspiring leader's assumptions about the type of curriculum that works for specific groups of students.

- How to develop safety net strategies to address the needs of struggling students. How to plan for students who enter without the prerequisite skills. How to lead differentiated classroom instruction. How to facilitate communication between specialists and general educators in the school.

- The importance of providing teachers with appropriate materials and adequate professional learning opportunities when a new curriculum is introduced.

- The use of replacement units to ease resistant teachers into new ways of doing things.

- The importance of bringing parents along early on in the process. How to work with them to promote an understanding of the rationale behind a particular curriculum choice, and how to manage parental anxiety about student capacity to master the curriculum.

How to Lead It When You Don't Know It

It is important, particularly for aspiring leaders and novice principals, to understand that while the role of the leader is often a lonely one, they do not need to know everything and do everything themselves. We make explicit the structures and models for distributing leadership around curriculum and professional learning and clarify the role of the principal in supervising them. In so doing we provide a transition from this course to the Instructional Leadership and Supervision course by addressing what to look for in a classroom visit.

Group Assignment

The class is broken up into small working groups. Each group is responsible for a curriculum content area, (e.g., English language arts, or mathematics), or a way of accommodating the curriculum for specific populations (e.g., students with special needs, English language learners), or a way of organizing curriculum (e.g., integrated curriculum, or curriculum mapping).

Each group is expected to design and present a forty-five minute professional learning experience in a specific curriculum area. Each presentation is expected to address:

- one or more of the state or local curriculum standards for the content area,
- and a strategy that presenters are expecting the audience (assumed to be teachers) to incorporate into their practice.

This assignment is intended to give aspiring leaders an opportunity to:

- make explicit their assumptions about the audience's prior knowledge, examine the basis upon which those assumptions have been made, and explore how to manage variability within the audience;
- experiment with what professional development strategies to employ to support their learning goals;
- think about how they will know if the audience has learned what they are teaching;
- and provide the class with the standard or curriculum framework for the content area and a list of resources—readings and materials—in the assigned curriculum area.

Aspiring leaders are expected to meet to develop these presentations outside of the class. Instructors meet at least once with each group, prior to the presentation to provide support and feedback during the planning process. Instructors focus on:

- the purpose of the presentation;
- use of time, pacing, and the information the presenters want the audience to come away with;
- the alignment of the information presented with the learning goals for the session;
- and the alignment of the professional development strategies with their educational philosophy and model for learning.

Individual Assignment

In addition to the group work, aspiring leaders are expected to lead a curriculum project, from the planning stage through completion, with adults in the school where they are currently working. This may be a group of colleagues or a group of parents—the important thing is that it be a group of adults. This assignment gives aspiring leaders an opportunity to practice making the transition from a focus on student learning to one of adult learning, and to see how adult behaviors affect student learning.

The project is broken down into four components:

- *Proposal or plan for the project*, including:
  - who the audience will be
  - the goal of the project
  - how this goal supports the teaching and learning in the school
  - what is expected to change as a result of the project, and how it will be measured or assessed
  - a brief description of the specific project activities, time frame, and resources required

  This component is intended to give aspiring leaders an opportunity to use planning as a learning process.

- *Professional reading.* Aspiring leaders are asked to select two articles or chapters from books that will deepen their knowledge of the curriculum area they have selected for their project. They are expected to write a "response" to each reading they have selected. This component is intended to engage aspiring leaders in critical thinking about curriculum issues.

- *Writing.* Aspiring leaders are asked to write two types of letters as part of their project. One is to parents describing the project goals, and one is to their project audience (typically, this is staff members who will participate in professional development), describing what the project will involve. Writing letters is an important part of the job of a principal, and this component is intended to give aspiring leaders an opportunity to practice their letter-writing skills.

- *Evaluation.* Aspiring leaders are asked to write an evaluative report describing what they believe worked and what did not work about the project, giving evidence for their opinion, and what they would change next time.

Aspiring leaders receive detailed feedback about each component of the project. They are given as many opportunities as they need to revise and refine their work. The objective of the instructors is to ensure that students leave the course with the skills these activities are designed to address.

URBAN SCHOOL COMMUNITY LEADERSHIP

Purpose

- to understand the relationship between the community outside of the school and the community inside the school

- to investigate the role of the school in the larger community and the place of the larger community in the school

- for future school leaders to be able to frame their schools as a community, and to leverage a community-based organization in support of their instructional mission

Instructors

This course is co-designed and taught by a university professor (ideally with an interest in school-community relations, theories of community and diversity, as well as experience with grant writing), and a practitioner (ideally a working principal or vice principal, at any level, with community-building expertise).

Session 1

Learning Goals

Introduction to the course. Review the following themes that will guide the work of the semester: (a) schools as communities; (b) schools and the broader communities in which they are located; (c) theories of community; (d) leadership in diverse community contexts; (e) historical developments in the New York City Board of Education; (f) parental involvement; (g) leveraging community resources; (h) and using research and evaluation to harness community support.

Frame

Schools and the communities in which they exist are inextricably interwoven. School leaders are challenged to address the demands of navigating and negotiating the community relationships within schools, and between the schools and other community institutions. Two key issues that emerge are (1) the role of schools in a capitalist democracy, and (2) the balance between the individual and the collective good. These issues are framed in terms of a commitment to equity in a diverse, urban context.

Additionally, the assignment that students will complete over the course of the semester (an actual grant application to a real foundation) is reviewed and discussed. As national and local scrutiny of public education intensifies, school leaders are asked to campaign for their schools, write grant applications for their schools, make community contacts on behalf of their schools, and publicly represent their schools. Their audiences range from boards of education to state legislatures, from the media to parents, and from industry representatives to community organizations. Through a course-long assignment requiring students to write grant applications (to be submitted to real foundations, corporations, and/or institutions), and to make presentations (to be delivered to authentic audiences), aspiring leaders develop their communication and fund-raising skills while applying for actual funding for their current schools or districts.

Activities

Instructors present an overview of the course. The class reviews the syllabus. Instructors review key concepts and theories of community that will frame the semester's discussion, including the work of Thomas Sergiovanni, Mara Sapon-Shevin, Amitai Etzioni, and Ferdinand Tonnies. The issues of equity, diversity, and the balance between the individual and the collective good are considered in terms of common school practices such as tracking or ability grouping. Other issues include the terms gifted, at-risk, and the various special education designations; bilingual education; communication with parents; navigating race and ethnicity; assessment programs; school choice programs; shared buildings; contractual arrangements; and parent involvement.

Students also participate in a community-building activity in which they each have a large piece of paper with four quadrants. The quadrants are as follows: your individual identity; the community or communities to which you belong; something that you have learned from the cohort community; and something that this community does not know about you that you are willing to share. Students are instructed to fill each quadrant with a graphic representation of themselves and their communities. Students then explain the drawings of themselves (or each other—we've done it both ways) to the rest of the class.

Debrief

Discussion of how after an entire semester of working together, we still learn new information about each other. Tie the exercise back to the issues of community, diversity, equity, and commonality, noting that by exchanging ideas and information, communities grow and develop.

Session 2

Learning Goals

This session has two main learning goals. The first is to explore theories of community and discuss how they relate to the organization of schools. Here, we pose the question of how schools might look if they were organized for equity, and the implications culled from the theories of community that we review. The second is to familiarize students with the Internet, how to use the Internet to search for possible resources for school-community collaborations and projects, and what the Internet means for our conceptualizations of the school community.

Frame

In a capitalist democracy, schools have the paradoxical roles of equalizing access to opportunity and reproducing a hierarchical labor force. Are schools intended to be reproductive or democratizing? What are the implications of this question, and the students' (often very divergent) answers, for theories of community?

Schools are often posited as a bridge from a *gemeinschaftlich* community to a *gesselschaftlich* society. We question whether this bridge is an appropriate metaphor for schools, and whether students believe that there are more appropriate metaphors. By analyzing school practices in terms of this framework, we can identify school practices that are out of sync with what students take to be the broader purposes of schooling. We can also think about practical ways in which school leaders might reorient practices to make them more consistent with their core beliefs and philosophies.

Activities

Whole class discussion facilitated by instructors.

Debrief

Applying the theories of community to specific practices and routines elucidates the assumptions built into many leadership decisions. Students are challenged to think through their own assumptions, ways of operating as teachers, and convictions about the role of schools and how they serve the communities in which they exist.

Readings

C. Merz and G. Furman. *Community and Schools: Promise and Paradox.* (1997)

The Foundation Center. *The Foundation Center's Guide to Proposal Writing*, 3d ed. (2001)

Session 3

Learning Goals

Prior to this session, students have all attended a school board meeting. The instructors provide a study guide for the meeting, and students take notes throughout its duration. The goals for this session are to revisit the question of the purpose of schooling for the child, the family, the community, the region, and the country. The school board meeting provides an anchor for that discussion and a focus on voice, language diversity, racial/ethnic diversity, and political power.

During this session, the instructors also introduce the grant-writing assignment, and tie it to the overarching theories and themes of the course. Students are encouraged to think about how they might devise programs or projects that connect their school with the larger community.

Frame

Is the creation of "community" in schools an end in and of itself? Is a strong community sufficient (independent of student learning and performance) for school success? How does instructional leadership fit into notions of community and the role of schools in a capitalist democracy? What are the tensions in community control, and the limits in representative politics?

Activities

Class discussion facilitated by instructors.

Debrief

Instructors again link the work and thinking for the grant assignment to the theoretical underpinnings of the class. Instructors also pose questions about how the school board meeting revealed power hierarchies that shape the community's sense of whose voice and opinions matter. The tacit knowledge and microtheories of cause and effect that all practitioners develop are made explicit as we dig deeper into the premises that drive our daily work.

Readings

D. McGrath and P. Kuriloff. "They're Going to Tear the Doors Off This Place: Upper Middle Class Parent School Involvement

and the Educational Opportunities of Other People's Children."
(1999)

Session 4

Learning Goals

The issues of diversity in urban education are often complex, multidimensional, painful, and emotional. Within the urban school, instructional leaders must develop a vocabulary for, and comfort level with, confronting issues of racism, homophobia, religious intolerance, sexism, classism, and other forms of oppression.

Many school practices silence dialogues about race and racism, reproduce status hierarchies, and pit oppressed communities against one another. Through active, sustained dialogue among diverse school constituents, strategies that approximate more equitable arrangements emerge.

Frame

Work on diversity is often disquieting, uncomfortable, and emotional. School leaders need to develop strategies for leading all school community members in productive, purposeful dialogue about the equity imperative within diverse learning communities.

Activities

Group discussion and activities facilitated by the instructors. Students practice talking about student performance data (disaggregated by race), and reflect on how their approaches to this conversation recreate or disrupt power hierarchies.

Debrief

The type of conversation, held during class, serves as a model for the conversations that school leaders need to facilitate in their schools.

Readings

L. Delpit. "Skills and Other Dilemmas of a Progressive Black Educator" and "The Silenced Dialogue." (1995)

M. Fine. "Silencing and Nurturing Voice in an Improbable Context: Urban Adolescents in Public School." (1989)

M. Pollack. "How the Question We Ask Most About Race in Education Is the Question We Most Suppress." (2001)

Session 5

Learning Goals

This session reviews the historical developments and current realities of governance in the New York City Board of Education now the Department of Education. Students learn structural strategies for community involvement that incorporate various approaches to maximizing diversity and assessing community- and school-based political power. Students also gain substantive knowledge of the current rules and regulations for leadership teams, including team composition, responsibilities, and procedures.

Frame

New York City's history of local control provides a framework for the current governance structure of leadership teams. Decentralized decision making and collective leadership require specific skill sets for school leaders. These skill sets include consensus-building and attention to multiple sides of an issue, while pushing forward an instructional agenda.

Activities

Group discussion facilitated by instructors. Role play of leadership team decision-making strategies.

Discussion of grant assignment and how to construct effective executive summaries.

Debrief

Leadership by committee necessitates an ability to bring various elements of the school community together for effective, collective decision making.

Readings

Board of Education of the City of New York. *The Chancellor's Plan for School Leadership Teams.* (1998)

D. Ravitch. *The Great School Wars: A History of the New York City Public Schools.* (1988)

Session 6

Learning Goals

In this session, we switch gears to focus our attention on the grant-writing project. Through discussions of the various projects that students are pursuing, we evaluate the representation of the school community in the proposal's problem/need statements.

Frame

When representing a school community in an attempt to get funding, resources, or support, school leaders must be cautious not to focus on deficits and deficiencies, and to focus instead on asset mapping and leveraging.

Activities

Discussion and workshop on problem statements. After discussion led by instructors, students work in teams on the problem/need statements for their grant proposals.

Debrief

In attempts to persuade funders and community members to support school-based programs, school leaders have to balance the communication of need with the communication of strength, asset, and possibility.

Readings

M. *Patton. Utilization-Focused Evaluation: The New Century Text,* Chapter 7. (1996)

Session 7

Learning Goals

In this session we discuss the implications of common schooling practices on community building. We focus primarily on issues of "gifted and talented" and "special education" to note how the use of school-based language, "educationese" and policy-driven labeling practices, can create insiders and outsiders within and among the school community. Aspiring leaders are challenged to think about how the inherited practices of student designations and categorical

PRINCIPAL TRAINING ON THE GROUND

programs influence their leadership practice. Students reflect on the types of dialogue that they will encourage and lead, so that focus is maintained on the equity imperative and the community imperative developed during the semester.

Frame

School leaders need to struggle with the implications of common school-based practices on notions of "equity" and "community." School leaders must address what Hugh Mehan calls the "politics of representation" (Mehan 1996) and the school-based vocabulary that reflects policy practices rather than sound educational or instructional approaches.

Activities

In a discussion facilitated by the instructors, students discuss and plan for the types of dialogues, school culture, and staff development they believe could help a school community overcome the forces influenced by "targeted" policies that can interrupt both the equity imperative and the community imperative. Students also work on their grant applications with the support of the instructors.

Debrief

A great deal of school-based vocabulary was generated from policies, and is now divorced from its origins in practice. School leaders need to constantly reorient the school practices so as to ensure that the vocabulary does not exclude certain community members (especially parents) from full participation in the school community.

Readings

H. Mehan. "Beneath the Skin and Between the Ears: A Case Study in the Politics of Representation," pp. 241–268. (1996)

M. Sapon-Shevin, *Playing Favorites: Gifted Education and the Disruption of Community,* Preface and Introduction, pp. xix–11. (1994)

Session 8

Learning Goals

Students learn how to develop theories of action for their grant projects. Students learn to make explicit their implicit theories of cause and effect in their grant applications, and to better articulate the rationale of their projects. They learn to link inputs to activities, activities to immediate outputs, immediate outputs to intermediate outcomes, and intermediate outcomes to ultimate goals.

Frame

Behind every project or program, there are microtheories of cause and effect. By articulating the various logical connections between the inputs and ultimate goals of a project, the project's design becomes more clear and effective.

Activities

Together, students map out a theory of action for ALPS. Then, they work on the theory of action for their individual grant projects.

Debrief

Through the development of a program's theory of action, the program's contours and rationale become more clear. Also, the microtheories that drive a number of programmatic decisions are tested for their logical progression from inputs to program goals.

Readings

M. Patton. *Utilization-Focused Evaluation: The New Century Text,* Chapter 10. (1996)

Session 9

Learning Goals

Students will learn to evaluate program effectiveness by designing evaluation protocols for their grant projects.

Frame

In order to know whether a community-building initiative, or any other education initiative is effective, one must learn to design evaluative mechanisms that assess whether a program or project reaches its desired goals.

Activities

Discussion of key evaluation options (e.g., qualitative, quantitative), concepts (e.g., inputs; outputs; relationships; hypotheses; and treatment and control groups), and measurement is led by instructors. Then, students break into groups to determine how they will collect data and measure whether or not their theory of action is supported by the program's actual implementation in their schools.

Debrief

The decisions one makes about program evaluation reflect key assumptions and priorities. Funders want to ensure that when they finance a project, they are doing one that has a mechanism to determine whether or not it works, and what needs to be done to ensure that ultimate goals are attained.

Readings

M. Patton. *Utilization-Focused Evaluation: The New Century Text,* Chapter 11. (1996)

Session 10

Learning Goals

Students learn the basics of program-driven budgeting for community-related initiatives through work on the budget section of their grant applications. They learn that there are basically four types of costs that support a grant-funded initiative: personnel, indirect costs, other than personnel services (OTPS, including supplies, materials, equipment, and travel), and matching costs (these may include personnel, space, equipment, materials, or cash). They also learn the importance of the budget narrative.

Frame

Students learn the logic behind program- or performance-driven budgeting in which an indicator of "need" (through student assessment data or other evidence of the need for a program) drives the program design, and then the resources are leveraged and aligned to support the initiative.

Activities

After a brief lecture on budgeting and cost factors, students draft budgets for their grant project. Students work either as individuals or in teams to determine all of the cost factors for their projects, and discern all of the associated costs. The instructors circulate, providing individual support to students as needed.

Debrief

This session is a preview of the budget and finance class that students take in the following semester. The logic of program- or performance-driven budgeting, or the move from assessment data, to program, to resource alignment, is expanded upon as students learn to budget for an entire school.

Session 11

Learning Goals

Students tie the grant-writing project back to the larger themes of community, diversity, commonality, and parental involvement in education.

Frame

As we work on the discrete pieces of the grant assignment, it is important to remember the broad themes of the course: the role of education in a capitalist democracy; the equity imperative; issues of diversity and commonality in urban, public schooling; different frames for understanding "community," parental involvement; and site-based collaborative governance in schooling. Each grant project should tie into and be born out of a solid sense of these issues. Students should be able to articulate with ease the implications their projects have for the school community, and community building in general.

Activities

Group discussion, facilitated by the instructors.

Debrief

The grant project is just one example of how school leaders can align their actions, resources, and activities with their overall instructional goals. Every decision that a school leader makes, especially in the projects and programs that she or he pursues, communicates to the broader school community what she or he values.

Session 12

Learning Goals

Students work on their grant assignments, as individuals and in groups.

Frame

Since the last two weeks involve presentations to grant officers from foundations, the students hone their grant assignments, tie up loose ends, and work on strategies for presenting their school communities in the most compelling light.

Activities

Students work in small groups on their grant assignments.

Debrief

We wrap this session up with some tips on pitching the grant to foundation program officers.

Session 13

Learning Goals

Students learn by delivering presentations to program officers from a major foundation. Students are expected to give persuasive presentations, represent their schools in ways that build on assets while communicating the need for funding, and to answer questions articulately.

Frame

Experiential, situated learning and simulations of practice are the most effective pedagogies for adult learners. When placed in a real situation in which they have to defend their grant projects to a program officer, students gain important insights into the priorities and ways of thinking found in the foundation world.

Activities

Half the students deliver their presentations to Ford Foundation program officers. Each presentation lasts ten minutes with five to ten minutes of Q & A from the program officers.

Debrief

Typically, the program officers and instructors provide an overall critique of the presentations. This critique usually focuses on the evaluation plans for the grant project, and how students will know whether or not their program was successful.

Session 14

The learning goals, frame, activities, and debrief are the same as Session 13. Also, we wrap up the course by tying the various themes and activities together.

LAW

We have struggled considerably with the positioning of the law course. We have had excellent lawyers teach courses on the fascinating world of education case law, but the courses did not prepare future principals for the ways in which they might need legal knowledge. We have also had practitioners involved in various aspects of educational law teach the course, but the focus tended to be too narrow, based on their daily work responsibilities. We have yet to strike the right balance between the immediate needs of our aspiring leaders, and the expertise and approach of those in the legal field. In fact, we have debated whether this course warrants an entire semester in the context of principal training. We would like to design a course that prepared school leaders for the various contractual issues faced when supervising teachers, as well as the federal, state, and court-mandated rights of students, parents, and teachers in the school system. Principals use some of this knowledge all of the time, and a lot of this knowledge on a need-to-know basis. We would like to teach principals enough about the laws that shape their interactions so that they will not complicate any legal issue that arises. We want them to understand the legal structures that govern their schools and shape their interactions with teachers, students, and parents; and help them explore how to lead instruction within this context. Since we have not crafted a version of this course that we are satisfied with as of this writing, we will not present detailed information on any particular syllabus. We are, of course, still trying to shape this course into one that supports future school leaders.

INTERNSHIP

While New York state has an internship requirement for school administration and supervision certification, the school district does not support a paid internship program. Aspiring leaders fulfill the internship requirement in the setting in which they are employed. Internship responsibilities are in addition to those of their regular jobs, and interns do not receive additional compensation for them. Although certainly not ideal, the close working relationship between the university and the district in support of this program has allowed us to maximize our students' learning opportunities within this context. That is, the district has been willing to provide release time so that aspiring leaders can make site visits to other schools, and attend seminars. They have taken on the responsibility for on-site supervision of the internship activities aspiring leaders are required to engage in at their schools, and they have provided sites for the on-site visit component of the program. These sites are selected by the district, either because they have implemented a unique approach, or because they are facing a specific challenge the district believes aspiring leaders should observe. In addition to their use in the internship program, these specific sites are used for in-depth case studies in the Instructional Leadership and Supervision course.

Purpose

The purpose of the internship component is to provide aspiring leaders with ongoing, hands-on experience in which they apply the knowledge they have gained in their coursework. The experiences aspiring leaders have during the internship are located in various settings: at their own schools, on visits to other schools, at the district's summer school program, and within the context of a focused seminar.

Location 1: Their Own Schools

Aspiring leaders engage in four sets of activities at their own schools:

- An ongoing experience of leading a project from start to finish (e.g., running a grade conference, working with parents on the new math curriculum), and a group of short-term experiences that they should have done at least once (e.g., ordering books and instructional materials).

- In addition, we wanted aspiring leaders to get a concrete sense of what a principal does. To do this, they shadow their principals on their supervisory classroom visits (called walk-throughs), and observe principals while they meet with professional developers, hold budget meetings, and meet with parents.

- When aspiring leaders apply to become principals, it is critical that they be able to walk through a school, assess it, and have some insightful things to say about it in a very short period of time. To sharpen their "eyes," aspiring leaders are asked to complete an asset map of their own school during the first half of the internship. The results of the asset map, along with other information, forms the basis for fulfilling the assignment to define goals and objectives in the second half of the internship.

Location 2: Visits to Other Schools

This is another opportunity for aspiring leaders to hone their observation skills. Each visit begins with an overview of the school by the host principals, and includes observations of classrooms and a discussion with the host principals and their staffs about what they have observed. It is an opportunity for aspiring leaders to get-inside-the-head of a principal, to see the work through her or his eyes, and to become acquainted with a range of approaches to school improvement. It is also an opportunity to demystify the transformational process as host principals reflect upon how long it took to make change, the challenges they faced, the mistakes they made along the way, and what they would do differently in hindsight.

Location 3: District Summer School

The district's summer program, designed to accelerate the learning of struggling students, provided us with an excellent opportunity for aspiring leaders to gain authentic, hands-on experience leading instruction. The university/district partnership made it possible for us to place aspiring leaders in summer supervisory positions, and to support them as they struggled to meet the challenge.

Location 4: Focused Seminars

There are a number of topics covered in other courses that aspiring leaders need to approach from a less theoretical, more practical perspective. We group these into the focused seminar component of the internship program. Some seminars are organized around tasks that principal leaders have to perform. Others provide an opportunity for deeper, more focused conversations about issues that principal leaders may confront. But whatever the topic, whatever the nature of the conversation, the seminars revolve around the question, what would you do as a principal, and why?

Goals and Objectives

The development of goals and objectives for the year is something that every principal in the district is required to do. The program provides aspiring leaders with hands-on experience in developing goals, objectives, and an action plan for one of the curriculum areas in the school in which they currently work. The goals and objectives and plan of action are expected to be real, that is doable, and something their principals can actually use as they develop the school-wide goals and objectives for the coming year.

Professional Development

There never seems to be enough time to cover all of the issues related to leading professional learning. This is an area in which we have found that spiraling the learning works best if it is done in response to conversations with the aspiring leaders. Some of the topics this seminar has covered in the past are listed below.

- when to use which form of professional development (e.g., workshops; individual coaching sessions; study groups; action research; grade and staff conferences; and curriculum planning meetings)
- how to ensure that the staff development in a school is consistent with the conditions for effective learning
- how to link professional development activities to the school's instructional focus for the year
- how to organize professional learning around the needs of students rather than the preferences of teachers; how to meet with teachers and develop their professional learning goals for the year; how to respect what they want to work on, and at the same time ensure that your goals for the school are addressed
- how to work with staff developers; how to make your expectations clear; how to map out what they are working on and with whom; how to know what you should be seeing in classrooms as a result of their work with teachers; and what to ask staff developers when you visit classrooms together
- how to use staff developers as your coach when you are observing a lesson in a subject in which you are not an expert
- how to match teachers with staff developers, and how to manage tensions between them
- how to manage teachers who are resistant to the idea of participating in professional development

Off on the Right Foot: Beginning the School Year

A number of the tasks that principals engage in at the beginning of the school year set the tone for what is to follow. Again, we have found that spiraling the learning works best if we are responsive to the pressing concerns of new leaders. Some of the topics we have covered in the past are:

- How to run the beginning of the school year staff conference
- How to get to know your teachers, parents, and district office administrators
- The purpose of a vision statement—a set of beliefs, guiding principles, and expectations that shapes every decision of every member of the school community; and that defines what the principal expects of the teachers, and what the teachers expect of students
- How to use the development of a vision statement (a collaborative process that is led by the principal) to define the characteristics of a learning environment that can sustain and support it; how to use these conversations to leverage dialogue about what the school does well, and what it needs to improve; and how to use this assessment to inform schoolwide professional learning for the year
- How to communicate that vision to the wider school community, how the language of the vision is embedded in every communication written and verbal, how everything a principal says and does sends a message about what she or he believes and expects
- How to use strategic conversations to challenge the underlying assumptions of members of the school community that may not be consistent with the vision
- How principals need to start the year with teachers knowing how the principal is going to assess or evaluate their work, and how the principal expects teachers to assess and evaluate the work of their students
- How principals keep track of the goals they have agreed upon with, and for, each teacher—what each teacher will be working on, how they will be working on it, how that work will be assessed, and how this type of accountability can be a model for how teachers hold students accountable for their work
- How to organize for this type of accountability, how to build regular meetings with each teacher into your calendar at the beginning of the school year, and keeping those appointments

- How to include in the master calendar the various administrative tasks for which principals are responsible, and regular meetings with staff developers, parents, the custodian, and district office administrator; as well as grade meetings, staff meetings, planning time, and meeting time with specialists working in your school

- How to establish a schoolwide code of behavior, how to lead discussions about how teachers respond to discipline problems

- The value of having a staff handbook that articulates the rules, expectations, codes of behavior, and approaches to problem solving; and how to develop one collaboratively with teachers and, where appropriate, with students and parents

- The importance of ensuring that teachers have what they need to do their job

- The value of scheduling one-on-one conversations with teachers in the fall to:

  - Discuss where each student in the class is in his or her work

  - What assessment the teacher is using to determine what each student knows and needs to learn next

  - How the teacher is using this information to inform his or her instruction

  - And, most importantly, what support the teacher needs from the principal

- The role of the principal in how the school is organized for teaching and learning, how they are set up physically, how the day is organized, how to arrive at a rhythm in the school that everyone is comfortable with and comes to expect

Supervisory Behavior

To engage aspiring leaders in discovering who they are as supervisors and leaders, we provide opportunities to explore how, as supervisors, they might respond to different situations in different ways.

We wanted to address head-on the fact that principals often have to say things that are difficult for teachers to hear. We wanted to provide aspiring leaders with opportunities to practice how to balance discussing those hard things with providing emotional support; to be supportive, but not so supportive that the teacher can't take constructive criticism. We also discuss how to be clear when their expectations are not being met, and how to pace feedback so that it is effective.

Applying for a Supervisory Position

All of the aspiring leaders will eventually apply for supervisory positions in the district. To demystify the process we give them an opportunity to practice and receive feedback on the skills they will need to be strong candidates. As part of the internship program, aspiring leaders complete application forms and participate in mock interviews. They learn how to pace their responses, what to do when they get stuck, and how to contextualize comments by gathering information about the school for which they are applying. As part of the district's selection process, candidates who are recommended by the school-based screening committee then participate in a purposeful school visit (or walk-through) with the superintendent and/or deputy. Aspiring leaders have the opportunity to practice this part of the process as part of the course on Instructional Leadership and Supervision.

Organizing for the Following Year

Another task that novice principals will face is organizing for the next school year. Teacher and student placement can often be a very delicate matter. Aspiring leaders explore various ways of going about these tasks, and assess them in relation to their philosophy of education. We ask, for example, how does your educational philosophy apply to student and teacher placement? If you are trying to achieve *balance* in a classroom, what do you really mean by that word? We ask them to think through what information they will need about students and teachers, to consider the research on the effect of teacher/student placement on student performance, and to think about how much involvement teachers should have in the process of programming a school; how much to factor in relationships between students, and between students and teachers; how to inform parents about the process; how to manage parental responses to student placement; and how to identify and manage mismatches when they occur.

Part of organizing for the following year is creating a master schedule or program. We found that this topic became so central to how principals organize for instruction and manage their budget that we developed a scheduling mini-course to cover this aspect of the program content.

INSTRUCTIONAL LEADERSHIP IN EDUCATIONAL ORGANIZATIONS

Purpose

The purpose of this course is to introduce participants to the challenge of instructional leadership in today's schools. Modern school leadership demands a unique combination of skills in organizational design and change management, fused with a detailed knowledge of teaching and learning. Using a combination of lectures, discussions, simulations, and experiential practice, this course aims to assist students in building the diverse set of skills and knowledge needed by school leaders. Through a semester-long project, students confront conditions similar to those a new principal faces as she or he takes on the position of instructional leader in an unfamiliar school. The school is one that students visit during their internship class. The team project is coordinated with assignments and class work in the "Introduction to School Finance" course.

The class is organized around the final group project. For this assignment, each group develops a focused plan for instructional improvement that links programmatic and structural changes to budgetary and human resource considerations. The project is broken down into components designed to engage and support students in an in-depth critical examination of instructional leadership within the context of a real school. Each component is modeled for students by instructors using a real model school. At the end of the semester, presentations are made to an audience composed of district office staff for comment and review.

Students are exposed to a diverse set of recent writings on school leadership and organizational development, and are given opportunities to apply these concepts to the task of principal leadership for school improvement. In addition, through a series of structured, written classroom observations, students develop the requisite skills for evaluating teacher performance, an important part of the supervisory role of principal leaders.

Session 1

- Instructors give an overview of the Instructional Leadership and Finance courses. They discuss the link between them and give students their final project working group assignments.

- Students engage in an activity designed to help them identify their own leadership style.

- Instructors lead a discussion about the characteristics of effective leadership and the need to cultivate a range of leadership strategies.

Session 2

- Students practice their classroom observation skills by viewing a videotaped lesson and, based upon it, practice writing up a formal teacher observation.

- Instructors present student performance data from the real school they will use to model the final project components. They engage students in the kind of data analysis they expect students to use in developing their instructional focus goals and objectives for their final project.

- Organized in working groups, students practice their analytic skills by identifying the model school's strengths, challenges, and trends. They discuss and, as a group, come to consensus about what the school should work on next. They select the instructional area of focus and develop expectations for student achievement gains in the area of focus.

- Based upon the information they have on the model school, students prepare questions for the various school constituencies they will interview in the following session.

Session 3

This session is conducted on site at the model school.

- In small groups, students interview representatives of various constituencies at the school, including: teachers, parents, staff developers, and administrators. Using the "Dynamic Dialogue" technique adapted from Dynamic Dialogue (Coffman and Saunders 2000), students look for signs of collaboration, the capacity to co-create, and adaptability in the school culture. They chart their findings along the following five axes.

  - *Feeling or Approach*—What is the feeling you get from the interviewees? What is the essence of what they are trying to express?

  - *Boundaries*—What do they feel included in? Excluded from? What or whom are they trying to protect?

  - *Undiscussables*—What are their hidden hard truths? What are the hidden contracts?

  - *Perspective*—What are their beliefs? What patterns or habits of mind do you see?

  - *Purpose*—What are they trying to do? What do they want? How do they go about getting it?

- In addition students review the results of a school culture survey conducted at the model school. The survey is based upon *What's Worth Fighting for in Your School?* (Fullan and Hargreaves 1996).

- Instructors model the development of a "socio-gram" and in groups students develop one for the model school using the information from the interviews and the culture survey. The socio-gram is used to help students identify ways to approach the instructional focus within the specific context of the school they are working in.

Session 4

- Students are given a second opportunity to practice their classroom observation skills using a videotape of a lesson. The program views the task of classroom observation and write-up as an essential supervisory skill and, as a result, students receive extensive feedback from instructors on these assignments.

- Instructors lead a discussion of Fullan's "lesson": Attack incoherence: Connectedness and knowledge creation are critical. They discuss ways in which the principal can promote coherence through systems integration and synthesis.

- Instructors lead a discussion of systems thinking as a way of making sense of what is happening in a school and talk about how to use those understandings to make change effectively.

- In pairs, students are invited to recall an experience in their professional career that illustrates one of the principles of systems thinking, such as "Small changes can produce big results." (See Senge, Kleiner, Roberts, Ross, and Smith 1994.)

- Instructors lead a discussion about how systems behave and how organizations (including schools) behave like systems.

- Students play the "chaos game," developed by Margaret Wheatley, which demonstrates how systems work. Students discuss the implications of the game for leading change in schools, and explore the idea that if the conditions or rules change, the outcome will change.

- Instructors lead a discussion of how to understand how the system currently works and how to use that information to leverage change.

- In small groups students practice creating a visual map of how the system in the model school works around the instructional focus they have collectively identified.

- Instructors lead a discussion of these systems maps and support students as they identify the leverage points for change.

Session 5

This session is a day-long session and takes place on site at the model school.

- In small groups students spend the morning observing classes.
- In the afternoon instructors conduct mock principal interviews with each student. They ask students to:
  - identify the patterns they saw in the classes they observed, and

- discuss one class in detail and identify how they would work with the teacher to improve his/her practice if they became principal of the school.

- While individual students are being interviewed their classmates are engaged in writing up a classroom observation based upon one of the classes they visited in the morning.

Session 6

This session addresses how principals identify, use, and expand upon the various organizational structures in place in a school and manage them to support and promote their instructional focus.

- In small groups, students analyze the structures (such as grade conferences, all-staff meetings, and common planning time) they observed in the model school. The analysis is based upon the interviews they conducted, survey information, and their visit to the school.

- Students are invited to think about additional structures that might be put in place to support the instructional focus.

- Instructors lead a discussion of how organizational structures are or can be used to support instructional improvement. They explore the limitations of structural change and discuss how to ensure that structures are effectively used to promote change.

- Based upon their understanding of how the school culture works in the model school, they talk about the difficulties that can be anticipated in making change and strategize about how a principal might respond to them.

Session 7

This session addresses the use of programming as a tool for instructional improvement. It explores the various options available to school communities at the elementary and secondary levels. Using information from the model school students practice reprogramming the school to support the instructional focus they have selected. Students discuss the pros and cons of various programming options in promoting instructional improvement in the school.

Session 8

This session addresses the concept of the learning organization—a community that is engaged in learning at every level.

- Using the triad derived from the work of Peter Senge (Senge et al. 1994; Senge et al. 2000)—Guiding Ideas, Theory, Methods and Tools, and Innovations in Infrastructure—and the process of orienting the system toward those points explored in the "chaos game," students investigate ways of developing a cycle of continuous instructional improvement based upon adult learning:
  - Instructors lead an exploration of the links between individual and organizational learning through the identification of feedback loops. They support students in learning to identify the relationship between formal and informal feedback structures.
  - Students investigate ways to amplify the leadership potential in a school organization by widening and deepening informal relationships.
  - Students talk about how to break down the barriers that prevent an organization from engaging in adaptive adult learning in response to student needs.
  - Students examine the ways the culture in the model school values (or sends the message that it doesn't value) adult learning. They identify the ways in which adult learning is linked to student learning in the model school.
  - Students discuss how to incorporate these ideas into the plans they are developing for their final project.

Session 9

This session addresses issues of accountability.

- Students are invited to explore their attitudes toward accountability.
- Using Peter Senge's learning process model (see *Schools That Learn* [Senge et al. 2000], page 26) instructors lead a discussion

of how all learning is based upon feedback loops and how, by linking the learning process to the orientation points (Guiding Ideas, Theory, Methods and Tools, and Innovations in Infrastructure), the learning process becomes accountable.

- Students break into their final project groups and explore how this might work in the schools they are basing their final project on.

- Instructors lead a conversation about how this perspective might change their attitude about accountability.

Session 10

This session addresses the role of relationship and conversation management in instructional improvement and cultural change. Using a role-play based upon a case study, students practice strategies for managing "difficult conversations" about resistance to change.

Session 11

Based upon *Leadership on the Line* (Heifetz and Linsky 2002), this session gives students an opportunity to practices a range of leadership strategies and pitfalls using simulation scenarios designed around: seeing the forest *and* the trees; thinking politically; orchestrating the conflict; giving the work back to those who own it; and holding steady in the face of resistance.

Session 12

This is a working session in which students have the opportunity to receive support for their final projects.

Sessions 13 and 14

These sessions are devoted to student presentation of their final projects before authentic audiences composed of administrators from participating district offices.

Final Project Assignments

Assignment 1—Data Analysis: Making Sense of the Numbers

Using the data for your case school,

- Identify
  - areas of strength (provide evidence).
  - areas the school needs to work on (provide evidence).
- Discuss the trends or patterns you see
- Tentatively identify an area you believe the school should work on next. Give your rationale.
- Describe the quantifiable gains the school can expect in:
  - one year. Give your rationale.
  - three years. Give your rationale.

Assignment Expectations

- *Scope:* Assignment should cover the full scope of data in both breath and depth. Data should be considered from a variety of points of view, for example, whole school, by grade, by student characteristics.
- *Analysis:* Assignment should address the meaning of the data. What can be inferred? What assumptions have been made? What conclusions can be drawn?
- *Reasoning:* Assignment should provide a coherent logic for your conclusions. Arguments should be supported by evidence.

Assignment 2—Instructional Focus

- Briefly describe what you have learned about your case school from the:
  - responses to the school culture survey
  - site visit interviews
  - site visit of case school
- Considering what you know about the school data from assignment 1 and what you have learned about your case school from the information described above:
  - What will be your instructional focus for the year? Why?
  - What will be your instructional focus for a three-year period? Why?

• How are the short-term and the longer-term focuses linked?

Assignment Expectations

Scope: Assignment should cover all sources of information. Assertions should be based upon concrete evidence.

Reasoning: Assignment should provide a logic for conclusions. Logic should link past behavior with future expectations.

Assignment 3—Indicators of Success

Now that you have selected your instructional focus, what are your expectations? What do you hope to accomplish?

• What are your quantitative objectives?

• What are your qualitative objectives?

• Short term—one year?

• Long term—three years?

How will you know if you have reached your objective? How will you know if you are on the right track? What will be your indicators?

• Quantitative

• Qualitative

• Interim—month-by-month

• Short term—one year

• Long term—three years

Assignment Expectations

Scope: Assignment should cover all aspects of the task—quantitative, qualitative, interim, short term and long term. Objectives should be achievable. Indicators should be accessible.

Reasoning: Assignment should address the logic of why you have selected specific objectives and indicators. Arguments should be based upon evidence.

Assignment 4—Change

- As the instructional leader in your case school, briefly describe your educational philosophy.

- Briefly discuss your change theory. How do you believe schools get better at what they do? How is your change theory linked to your educational philosophy?

- What changes do you want to make in your case school? Why have you selected them?

- How will these changes affect your instructional focus? Over the short term? Over the long term?

Assignment Expectations

Scope: Assignment should be complete.

Reasoning: Assignment should reflect a coherent logic linking educational philosophy and change theory. Assignment should provide a rationale for the proposed change.

Assignment 5—Strategy

- Briefly describe how the current "system" works now with regard to your instructional focus.

- Provide a diagram.

- Describe how you will use this information to make the changes you propose.

Assignment Expectations

Scope: Assignment should be complete. Assignment should utilize the concepts and tools discussed in class.

Reasoning: Assignment should provide a coherent logic for the strategy. Arguments should be based upon evidence.

Assignment 6—Plan

Based upon assignments 1–5, complete an action plan for each of the changes you propose to make. Briefly describe each activity, who is responsible for it, and when it is scheduled to take place.

Assignment Expectations

Scope: Assignment should be complete and comprehensive.

Reasoning: Assignment should be consistent with previous assignments.

Assignment 7—Presentation

Provide a brief (no more than fifteen-minute) presentation of your plan, your rationale for it and its budget implications. Presentations should include:

- Where the school is now
- What you want to change and why
- How you propose to make the changes
- How you will measure success
- Resource implications
- Budget
- Human resources

For any given assignment, you can receive one of three possible grades:

E—Excellent (equivalent to an A)

S—Satisfactory (equivalent to a B)

R—Needs Revision (grades that are not revised by the end of the term can receive no better than a C)

Readings

A. Boyle. *Turning Failing Schools Around: Intervention in Inverse Proportion to Success.* (2001)

R. DuFour. "The Learning Centered Principal." (2002)

R. F. Elmore. *Leadership of Large-Scale Improvement in American Education.* (1999)

———. *Time Is Money That Has Been Spent.* (Dec. 2001)

————. *Leverage Points and Improvement Strategies.* (Jan. 2002)

————. *Leverage Points and Improvement Strategies: Continued.* (Feb. 2002)

E. Fink and L. Resnick. "Developing Principals as Instructional Leaders." (2001)

M. Fullan. *Leading in a Culture of Change.* (2001)

————. *What's Worth Fighting for in the Principalship?* (1997)

M. Fullan and C. Rolheiser. "Dealing with Resistance." (2001)

L. Gewirtzman and E. Fink. "Realignment of Policies and Resources." (n.d.)

R. A. Heifetz and M. Linsky. *Leadership on the Line: Staying Alive Through the Dangers of Leading.* (2002)

P. M. Senge. "The Leader's New Work: Building Learning Organizations." (1990)

Senge et al. "A Primer to the Five Disciplines." *Schools That Learn: A Fifth Discipline Fieldbook for Educators, Parents, and Everyone Who Cares About Education.* Chapter 2 (2000)

J. P. Spillane, R. Halverson, and J. B. Diamond. "Investigating School Leadership Practice: A Distributive Perspective." (2001)

D. Stone, B. Patton, and S. Heen. *Difficult Conversations: How to Discuss What Matters Most.* (1999)

INTRODUCTION TO SCHOOL FINANCE, A.K.A. GREEN DOLLAR BUDGETING

The district allocates resources to schools in the form of dollars, as opposed to positions. Within the constraints of law, regulation, and contractual agreements, principals and their leadership teams can determine how those resources are used. Aspiring leaders learn how to manage their resources in such a way that they were used effectively and efficiently to support their instructional agenda. We call this approach *green dollar budgeting*. The program drives the dollars rather than the other way around. To do this type of budgeting, aspiring leaders need to understand enough about the rules governing the funding sources to match them to their program needs. When they cannot make the match (that is, when the type of the funding source cannot be used for a specific purpose they feel is important to their instructional agenda), they learn how to negotiate funding switches with the district's budget office where possible.

This is a case where the learning is almost entirely in the doing. The course is structured around the development of a budget for a real school to support the school improvement plan that cohort members have developed for it in their "Instructional Leadership and Supervision" course. The schools for which these plans and budgets are developed are ones to which the aspiring leaders have made site visits as part of their internship program. In the process of working through the issues in this project, aspiring leaders become familiar with:

- the equity vs. equality issues implicit in the way the district constructs formulas to fund schools
- the rules governing various funding sources
- basic purchasing rules
- and some tips on how to stay out of trouble with the auditors

As a result of our experience having aspiring leaders produce one product, a school improvement plan for two courses—"Instructional Leadership and Supervision" and "School Finance"—we are beginning to experiment with integrating the curriculum more fully into a combined, six-credit course (rather than two three-credit courses). It is our hope that by doing so the course structure will more closely mirror how we would like novice principals to approach budgeting—as a support for (rather than as the driver of) their instructional improvement goals.

Mini-courses

In addition to the fourteen-session, credit-bearing courses the program offers we have found it useful to run a series of one-day, intensive mini-courses about topics such as:

- "Assessment Literacy"—what the assessment tools you use can, and cannot, tell you about what your students know and are able to do
- "Making Time—Creative Programming and Scheduling"
- "Looking at Student Work"
- "How to Organize for Action Research"
- "The Role of Special Education in Your School"
- "The Role of English as a Second Language Instruction in Your School"
- "Demystifying the Teacher's Contract"

SAMPLE ASSIGNMENT RUBRICS

Administration of the Urban School

Action Plan

A formal document that describes an approach to solve a school-based problem. The plan typically includes a narrative that defines the problem, a plan for addressing the important components of the problem (including specific activities, their sequence, research-based rationale, personnel responsible, and overall timeline for completion). It also includes strategies for gaining support of the key players involved and for overcoming expected obstacles. (See rubric for assessment criteria.)

Final Reflection (End of Semester)

A chance to write about the organization of the class, your role as a future leader, your interactions with your colleagues, and the assigned readings. You should integrate the experiences and information from all three cases into a cohesive narrative.

Group PowerPoint Presentation (Cases 2 and 3)

An oral presentation to an invited audience in which various group members take responsibility for a section of the presentation and all group members field questions. You will use PowerPoint, a computer software program that allows presenters to organize ideas and images. Each class member will make a presentation (as part of a group) using PowerPoint during the course of the semester. (See rubric for assessment criteria.)

In-Basket Exercise (Case 1)

A pivotal, hands-on experiential class session in which we simulate a day in the life of a principal. Each student will be handed a stack of papers from a typical principal's "to-do" list and will have the duration of the class period to complete all activities. There will be live interruptions during the exercise.

Letter to the Community (Cases 1, 2, and 3)

An opportunity to communicate with your school community about your plans for action based on each case. The letter should weave together your best thinking about the direction you think the school should take, based on the in-class experiences, group-work processes, presentations, and readings. The letter should demonstrate your ability to think critically, to integrate the readings and experiences into your writing, and to communicate effectively with various segments of the school community. (See rubric for assessment criteria.)

Online Communication

A method for communicating with classmates and group members in cyberspace. Each class member will be given access to an online discussion forum where you will be expected to engage in discussion in preparation for your face-to-face meetings. There is an online communication assignment for each case, but you are free to use it beyond the required communication toward your grade. (See rubric for assessment criteria.)

Talk-Back Sheet

An optional opportunity for you to express what you found useful in each case and how you think it could be improved in its future use. You can say as much, or as little, as you like on the talk-back sheets; these are intended to be constructive venues for sincere efforts at continual improvement. The talk-back sheets are not graded.

Vision

A future-oriented portrait that captures the hopes, values, and goals of your school. Simply stated, a vision is what you want your school to look like. A school's vision should constantly evolve in response to new realities.

Rubrics

Your work will be assessed using the following rubrics. E = Excellent, S = Satisfactory, R = Rewrite, F = Fail.

Action Plan: 5 Page Maximum

Grade	Substance (2/3 of final grade)	Style (1/3 of final grade)
E	• clear, logical narrative that concisely states the problem and its components.	• clear organization
	• thoughtful and thorough discussion of the significance of the problem	• writing is concise, persuasive, and effective
	• a detailed, organized, and logical plan that consistently addresses the problem and contains relevant sample activities (in an appendix—sample activities do not count toward the five-page maximum)	• no more than a total of three of the following:
		(a) typos, misspellings, or grammatical errors
		(b) "common errors" such as it's/its, use of contractions, that/which, gender specificity, effect/affect, use of "etc.," or use of abbreviations
	• considerable integration of group research and practice to address the problem and rigorous analysis of case details	
	• substantial consideration of obstacles, alternative perspectives, and solutions	
	• solutions and strategies that are research-based and grounded in current notions of best practice	

Grade	Substance (2/3 of final grade)	Style (1/3 of final grade)
S	• mostly clear and logical narrative that states the problem and its components	• clear organization
	• some discussion of the significance of the problem and analysis of case details	• writing is persuasive and effective
	• un organized and logical plan that addresses the problem and contains relevant sample activities (in an appendix—sample activities do not count toward the five-page maximum)	• no more than a total of six of the following:
		(a) typing, misspellings, or grammatical errors
	• some integration of group research and practice to address the problem	(b) "common errors" such as it's/its, use of contractions, that/which, gender specificity, effect/affect, use of "etc.," or use of abbreviations
	• some solutions and strategies that are research-based and grounded in current notions of best practice	
R	• very loose organization and minimal analysis	
	• response to problem/challenge posed in assignment	
	If you do not meet the S or E standard, you will be asked to rewrite your action plan. If you choose not to rewrite, you will receive a grade of C or lower.	

Grade	Substance (2/3 of final grade)	Style (1/3 of final grade)
F	• Any form of academic dishonesty	• direct quotation of published or unpublished author without proper citation; representation of another's words as if they were your own, without proper citation; submission of work that is not your own original work.

Final Reflection

There is no rubric for this assignment. You will get full credit for submitting a thoughtful piece that incorporates the various learning experiences that you had in this class and how they inform your thinking about educational leadership.

Group PowerPoint Presentation

Grade	Substance (2/3 of final grade)	Style (1/3 of final grade)
E	• clear organization with logical progression between thoughts and ideas • rigorous analysis of assignment question indicating considerable reflection and close consideration of case information and available resources • evaluative, research-based support for arguments, perspectives, propositions, and plans	• use of Power-Point and handouts that supports your presentation rather than detracts from it • clean, sharp use of graphics and animation that is easy to follow and facilitates communication • group members come across as "one voice" • entire formal presentation takes up no more than the allotted time

Grade	Substance (2/3 of final grade)	Style (1/3 of final grade)
E *(continued)*	• presentation demonstrates in-depth understanding of audience concerns, expectations, and understandings • clear responses to audience questions that demonstrate understanding of the questions and thoughtful consideration of audience members' concerns	• PowerPoint slides and handouts have no typos, misspellings, or grammatical errors
S	• mostly clear organization with logical progression between thoughts and ideas • sound analysis of assignment question indicating reflection and consideration of case information and available resources • support for arguments, perspectives, propositions, and plans • presentation demonstrates understanding of audience concerns, expectations, and understandings • clear responses to audience questions that demonstrate understanding of the questions and consideration of audience members' concerns	• PowerPoint slides and handouts have no more than four typos, misspellings, or grammatical errors • entire formal presentation takes up slightly more than the allotted time • otherwise, same as for an E

Grade	Substance (2/3 of final grade)	Style (1/3 of final grade)
R	• very loose organization and minimal analysis *If your group does not meet the S or E standard, you will be invited to a meeting with the professors to discuss your group's processes and strategies for future presentations/group work. After this meeting, you will be asked to redo the PowerPoint slideshow to hand in (rather than deliver). If you do not attend the meeting, or your group does not turn in a revised version, you will get a C or lower.*	
F	• any form of academic dishonesty	direct quotation of published or unpublished author without proper citation; representation of another's words as if they were your own without proper citation; submission of work that is not your own original work.

Letter to Community: 2 Page Maximum

Grade	Substance (2/3 of final grade)	Style (1/3 of final grade)
E	• clear organization with logical progression between thoughts and ideas • careful consideration of your audience, the case situation, and your own position as a new administrator • response to problem/challenge posed in case (rather than some other topic of your invention) • response shows critical thinking and creativity • rigorous analysis of problem/challenge indicating considerable reflection and consideration of course themes • support for arguments, perspectives and propositions from professional literature	• paragraph organization with topic sentences and smooth transitions between ideas • tone appropriate for audience • no more than one of the following: (a) typos, misspellings or grammatical errors (b) "common errors" such as it's/its, use of contractions, that/which, gender specificity, effect/affect, use of "etc.," use of abbreviations • writing style is appropriate for audience (graduate-level professors and professionals)

Grade	Substance (2/3 of final grade)	Style (1/3 of final grade)
S	• organization with logical progression between thoughts and ideas • some integration of professional literature and your own thoughts • response to problem/challenge posed in assignment	• no more than five of the following: (a) typos, misspellings or grammatical errors (b) "common errors" such as it's/its, use of contractions, that/which, gender specificity, effect/affect, use of "etc.," use of abbreviations • writing style is appropriate for audience (graduate-level professors and professionals)
R	• very loose organization and minimal analysis • response to problem/challenge posed in assignment *If you do not meet the S or E standard, you will be asked to rewrite your paper. If you choose not to rewrite, you will receive a C or lower.*	• more than five typos, misspellings, grammatical errors, or "common errors" (as noted above) • inappropriate or inconsistent tone for audience
F	• any form of academic dishonesty	• direct quotation of published or unpublished author without proper citation; representation of another's words as if they were your own without proper citation; submission of work that is not your own, original work.

Online Communication

Grade	Standard

E
- thoughtful reflection on assigned question
- response that reflects clear command of the readings
- engagement with the ideas reflected in your colleagues' postings

S
- reflection on assigned question
- response that reflects familiarity with the readings

R
- response to question that does not demonstrate command of the readings

If you do not meet the S or E standard, you will be asked to meet with the professor(s) to discuss whatever obstacles you are facing.

F
- any form of academic dishonesty

•NOTE At times, assignments cannot be posted by the due dates, because of technological difficulties. When messages cannot be posted, due to factors outside of the students' control, their grades will not reflect strict adherence to this rubric in terms of assignment timeliness. However, when the system is working (and it usually is), all class participants are expected to post online assignments by the due dates.

PARTICIPANTS' STORIES

Following is a view of the program from the perspective of Carmen Farina, superintendent of Community School District 15:

> As a new Superintendent, one of the most pressing issues I faced was the lack of leadership candidates who are able to think creatively and outside the box. Having come from a district where both of these qualities were held in high regard, it was important to find a program that could in a short period of time turn out well-trained and sophisticated school leaders. By having our candidates participate in the Baruch ALPS program, we were able within a year's time to not only fill positions, but change the level of leadership that demonstrates the district's educational and leadership philosophy.
>
> In addition to providing practical, up-to-date school experiences, it encouraged strong networking among the participants. This networking made it possible for people who entered the program with a variety of experiences to share their expertise with each other. In one of the cohort groups there was a district office administrator, several guidance counselors, some teachers and a staff developer. By sharing the unique perspective with each other all of these candidates not only became better leaders, but also supported each other throughout the year as specific issues came up in their daily work life. This program also allowed us to put these prospective leaders in a position to run summer school programs and give them a better feeling for the day-to-day challenges of the school world. I believe that because of their specific training they were all able to rise to the challenge in an exemplary fashion. Our specific success stories have been the candidates that were not teachers but were guidance counselors wishing to

become administrators. These candidates possessed excellent people skills but lacked the curriculum expertise that is so crucial to strong school leadership. By providing each of these candidates with an intense on-site curriculum internship, we were able to assure ourselves of strong leadership for the future. The ALPS Program is the only one I know of that truly duplicates the real world of school leadership with challenging and high level classroom assignments. It also fosters collegiality among future leaders; something that other programs do not place a high value on. Most importantly, an overwhelming number of those participating in this program are applying for leadership positions in the fall.

Below is a view of the program from the perspective of a novice principal, Rhonda Perry, of the Salk School of Science in Community School District Two:

In my mind, the glue that held all of the courses in the Aspiring Leaders Program together was the consistent and unrelenting focus on instruction and community. Perhaps the most essential message I took away from the program is the understanding that all decisions made in a school must have the aim of improving or maximizing the quality of instruction in the classroom. Egos must be cast aside, professional isolation must be fought, blame and excuses must become unacceptable—all facets of school culture and relationships within the building must be closely examined in order to build an environment that fosters learning and growth for everyone, especially children. To create a culture of intellectual curiosity within a school, I learned that the principal must be a reflective learner—continually becoming, forever striving to foster her own learning life, committed to the principles of democracy and teamwork, and willing to believe or imagine things into being.

How did the ALPS program nurture these ideas? When you put insightful professors and reflective principals together with a group of brilliant teachers in a program designed to foster conversation—well, nothing but magic can happen. It was a privilege to be in conversation with some of the best teachers in the system, pouring over cases, exchanging ideas about the best literature on school leadership, viewing best practice in purposeful classrooms and schools, apprenticing ourselves to the best principals, and hearing from the best leaders in the school system. I felt alive and challenged, learning and thinking with other educators who were already striving to be all they could for the children they taught. I understood by the end of the program that the work of the principal is to create an environment where teachers feel valued and intellectually stimulated and to keep instruction at the heart of every decision. The job of the principal is to forever strive to be the best teacher.

And lastly, here is the program from the perspective of a program graduate, Katherine Casey, who is now teaching in the Educational Leadership Development Academy (ELDA) in San Diego, CA:

"What have we gotten ourselves into? How will we ever learn enough to become principals? How will we take coursework, complete an internship, and teach children simultaneously? And, what *is* problem-based learning?" These refrains punctuated conversations among cohort members during our first weeks in ALPS. Like many of my cohort members, I did not enter ALPS because I had a burning desire to become a principal, or because I had sought out an administration program, and I did not have much understanding of what the program would entail. I applied to ALPS at the urging (insistence, actually) of my principal, who, from time to time over two years, mentioned administration programs, explained to me why I should further my education, and listened patiently as I dismissed her suggestions with, "I am quite happy as a classroom teacher" or "There is no way I could ever feel ready to be a principal." Despite my resistance, my principal gave me an application to ALPS, informed me that my superintendent and math mentor both agreed that I should apply, and handed me her written recommendation. Across the nation, the alarming lack of qualified applicants for instructional leadership positions is causing outstanding leaders in districts to do exactly what my principal did—identify people with potential and cajole them into administration programs. Boosted by words of encouragement from my respected leaders and mentor, I applied to ALPS and thrived on the rigor and outstanding teaching and learning opportunities.

I point to ALPS as an incredibly powerful and transformational burst of learning that continues to reverberate. I have experienced and scrutinized ALPS from four vantage points: as a graduate of the Baruch College New York City Schools Program, as a
co-developer of an iteration of the program at the University of
San Diego—San Diego Unified Schools Education Leadership
Development Academy (ELDA), as an instructor in the Tier I
ELDA program for people becoming administrators, and as an
instructor and support provider for administrators continuing
their leadership education in the Tier II ELDA program.

ALPS was such a powerful and successful experience for me
because the program is crafted around a common sense yet rarely
realized principle: to prepare for a real job, people must learn how
to tackle the demands of the real job.

- The content of our coursework balanced theory and reality.
  How will we ever learn enough to become principals?—by
  engaging in real learning and making the unknown known.
  Our course projects utilized real situations and data and
  required us to face and tackle scenarios with real problems
  that face school administrators. For example, we learned
  about the theory of school finance and then we got our hands
  on real budget grids and had to design a budget for our
  school, shifting the murmurs to, "this is how I could do it if
  I were a principal." The unforgettable "in-basket" experience
  required us to problem-solve our way through the type of
  paperwork a principal faces every day.

- Our courses were co-taught by a professor and a practitioner.
  So often a rich theoretical conversation turned to an equally
  rich practical conversation about how the theory played out
  on a daily basis in a school. Guest speakers from the district—newer principals, more experienced principals, the
  budget director, a member of the team who reviews union
  grievances—gave advice, explained reality, and, as importantly, became known to us so that in our future roles, we
  could turn to them for information and support.

- Much of our learning occurred in cooperative groups or
  teams to mirror the reality of shared decision making in
  school leadership. We learned to work through the challenges
  of working as a team. We made and corrected mistakes with

each other that could have damaged us in our first years as principals. Because we spent the entire year together as a cohort, we developed the necessary support network that could sustain us in the relatively isolated role of school leader.

• The program required us to complete an internship and expected us to use experiences from our internships to shape our understanding of the coursework. The internship immersed us in the daily tasks of the principalship. We learned as we worked alongside mentor principals, we engaged in work as principal interns in our schools, we observed real lessons, gave live feedback to teachers in our schools, lead professional development, received feedback from our ALPS mentor, created budgets for our schools, and so on.

From my vantage point now I hear our ELDA members whisper, "What have we gotten ourselves into?" as I work with my colleagues and continually ask, "What have we gotten ourselves into? How will we ever do enough to help them become principals with increasing amounts of knowledge and skill? What is the most effective coursework, internship experience, on-the-job training? And what *are* the best cases for problem-based learning?" My involvement with co-developing the ELDA program has impressed upon me how rare ALPS is (how lucky I was to be encouraged to apply to it since I now know what most administrative programs offer) and how difficult it is to build a collaborative relationship between school districts and universities to actually realize a program based on that common sense principal: To prepare for a real job, people must learn how to tackle the demands of the real job.

AFTERWORD

When we first tried to "grow our own" school leaders in District Two, the set-up was far from ideal; we had little money to spend, and not much direct experience in creating a joint program with a university partner like Baruch College. Even so, as Liz and Sandra explain in the foregoing chapters, we found a way to make the pieces fit together.

The pieces that need to be pulled together to create a program like ALPS are different in every school district; the university partner, the district's own approach to instruction, the processes for selecting and supervising principals, the budget, and the broader political context are just a few of the factors that come into play. Those elements came together in New York because of our shared focus on adult learning, our commitment to collaboration, our eagerness to develop the strongest possible program, and a coherent approach to school leadership and instruction.

The Educational Leadership Development Academy, or ELDA, launched in San Diego in 2000 by the San Diego City Schools and the University of San Diego, draws heavily on lessons from ALPS. Like ALPS, ELDA is a co-constructed program that mixes theoretical and practical approaches, requires strong collaboration between the school system and the university, and depends on problem-based learning. Yet ELDA is also a very different program. Some differences are simply the result of applying the model in a different school system—one in the midst of a comprehensive program of school reform; others represent intentional shifts of emphasis and improvements on the ALPS model.

The key distinction between ALPS and ELDA is the status of the San Diego program as a full-fledged academy, with its own executive director within the school of education of the University of San Diego. ELDA not only trains aspiring principals, but coaches them during their early years as school leaders and supports the professional learning of the district's principals and their supervisors— the instructional leaders. In New York, by contrast, ALPS is a more loosely coordinated training program, with ongoing supervision and professional development of administrators remaining within the school system. ELDA's hybrid approach has given added coherence to the San Diego school system during a period of profound instructional change.

Other differences show how basic program elements can be applied and developed differently in a new situation. In San Diego, for example, we have been able to give aspiring principals a full year's internship with exceptional supervising principals. At the same time, we offer our interns a program of coursework taught collaboratively, as in the ALPS program, by university instructors and practitioners, and involve them in critique and discussion of their own work and that of their colleagues. Because the internships are closely supervised by ELDA, the connection between the internships and the coursework is strong and immediate. Through experiential learning, the interns develop a specific set of essential leadership skills and receive a high level of attention to their individual growth as leaders. In addition, ELDA coaches the supervising principals—a process that sharpens their skills as principals and mentors.

In San Diego, we have also put a great deal of emphasis on the use of video as an instructional tool for leaders at all levels. Instead of merely reading and talking about practice and analyzing problems in the abstract, San Diego interns, principals, instructional leaders, and other supervisors are able to practice leadership behaviors, observe their own performance on video, and discuss their work in detail with their instructors and colleagues. I cannot emphasize enough how powerful this has been. Video has opened the eyes of many people to discrepancies between what they think they were doing and how they actually perform leadership tasks—a first step in analysis, replanning, and professional growth. The method has also changed the way we give and receive criticism, since all of us have had the experience of having our work videotaped and discussed.

I should point out that we have altered the ELDA model over time, as opportunities and problems have arisen. For example, after learning that principals were receiving contradictory messages from instructional leaders and the district's literacy and math departments, we decided to bring both groups together to plan principals' conferences that integrate the district's curricular goals. Interestingly, the discipline involved in co-constructing the conferences has produced stronger, more coherent, and better thought out sessions. Also, as former participants in the internship program began to move into principalships, we added a second tier of support for new school leaders through a structured program of mentoring and school visits, conducted jointly by ELDA and the instructional leaders. Over time, ELDA has refined its collaboration with the instructional leaders to ensure that we continuously improve our ability to support new principals and help them increase their effectiveness as the leaders of adult learning in their schools.

The real message of all this work is that it requires great creativity, flexibility, and inventiveness to develop and sustain a program capable of training principals to meet the steep challenges of school leadership today. To succeed, such a program needs to draw on and integrate theory and practice, foster collaboration between practitioners and professors, find constructive ways to give encouragement and criticism, and emphasize both coherence and innovation. A problem-solving strand runs through the coursework of both ALPS and ELDA—the same kind of problem solving that lies at the heart of our own efforts to design the programs and make them work. Other school systems will undoubtedly adopt their own unique strategies to develop school leaders, but the planners of those programs, like today's public school principals, must be ready to solve problems and learn rapidly at every step.

ELAINE FINK
EXECUTIVE DIRECTOR, EDUCATIONAL LEADERSHIP ACADEMY,
SAN DIEGO CITY SCHOOLS;
FORMER SUPERINTENDENT AND DEPUTY SUPERINTENDENT
NEW YORK CITY COMMUNITY SCHOOL
DISTRICT TWO

BIBLIOGRAPHY

American Association of Colleges for Teacher Education. 2001. *PK–12 Educational Leadership and Administration*. Online and available at: www.aacte.org/Membership_Governance/edleadership.pdf.

Argyris, C. 1986. "Skilled Incompetence." *Harvard Business Review* (September–October).

———. 1991. "Teaching Smart People How to Learn." *Harvard Business Review* (May–June).

Argyris, C., and D. A. Schön. 1974. *Theory in Practice: Increasing Professional Effectiveness*. San Francisco: Jossey-Bass.

Axelrod, R., and M. D. Cohen. 2000. *Harnessing Complexity: Organizational Implications of a Scientific Frontier*. New York: Basic Books.

Bangs, D. H. Jr. 1998. *The Business Planning Guide: Creating a Plan for Success in Your Own Business*. 8th ed. Chicago: Upstart.

Berns, R. G., and P. M. Erickson. 2001. "Contextual Teaching and Learning: Preparing Students for the New Economy." In *The Highlight Zones: Research @ Work, 5*. Department of Education, National Center for Career and Technical Education. Online and available at: www.nccte.org/publications/infosynthesis/highlight-zone/highlight05/index.asp.

Board of Education of the City of New York. 1998. *The Chancellor's Plan for School Leadership Teams*. Online and available at www.nycenet.edu/govern/governancedece/default.htm.

Borko, H., and R. Putnam. 1998. "The Role of Context in Teacher Learning and Teacher Education." In *Contextual Teaching and Learning: Preparing Teachers to Enhance Student Success in and*

Beyond School, pp. 35–74. Columbus, OH: ERIC Clearinghouse on Adult, Career, and Vocational Education; and Washington, DC: ERIC Clearinghouse for Teaching and Teacher Education, ED 427263. www.contextual.org.

Boyle, A. 2001. *Turning Failing Schools Around: Intervention in Inverse Proportion to Success.* London: Leannta Education Associates.

Bransford, J. D., A. L. Brown, and R. R. Cocking, eds. 1999. *How People Learn: Brain, Mind, Experience, and School.* Washington, DC: National Academy Press.

Bridges, E., and P. Hallinger. 1994. *Problem-Based Learning— Time Management.* Educational Resources Information Center. ISBN: 0-86552-171-1.

———. 1995. *Implementing Problem-Based Learning in Leadership Development.* Eugene, OR: ERIC Clearinghouse.

Brown, A. L., and A. S. Palincsar. 1989. "Guided, Cooperative Learning and Individual Knowledge Acquisition." In *Knowing, Learning, and Instruction: Essays in Honor of Robert Glaser,* ed. L. B. Resnick, pp. 393–451. Hillside, NJ: Erlbaum Associates.

Bryk, A. S., J. Q. Easton, D. Kerbow, S. G. Rollow, and P. A. Sebring. 1993. *A View from the Elementary Schools: The State of Reform in Chicago.* Chicago: Steering Committee of the Consortium on Chicago School Research.

Cambourne, B. 1998. *The Whole Story: Natural Learning and the Acquisition of Literacy in the Classroom.* New York: Scholastic.

Capra, F. 2002. *The Hidden Connections: Integrating the Biological, Cognitive, and Social Dimensions of Life into a Science of Sustainability.* New York: Doubleday.

City University of New York, Baruch College. n.d. *Graduate Bulletin 2001–2003.* New York: Baruch College Office of Communications and Marketing.

Coffman, B., and M. Saunders. 2000. "Dynamic Dialogue." Presentation at the Systems Thinking in Action Conference, 23–25 October.

Comings, J., B. Garner, and C. Smith, eds. 2000. *Annual Review of Adult Learning and Literacy, 1.* Project of the National Center for the Study of Adult Learning and Literacy. San Francisco: Jossey-Bass.

Daresh, J. C. 1997. "Improving Principal Preparation: A Review of Common Strategies." *NASSP Bulletin* 81 (585): 3–8.

Darling-Hammond, L. 1997. *Why Teaching Matters.* Report of the National Commission on Teaching and America's Future. New York: September 1996.

Delpit, L. 1995. "Skills and Other Dilemmas of a Progressive Black Educator" and "The Silenced Dialogue." In *Other People's Children: Cultural Conflict in the Classroom.* New York: New Press.

Donaldson, M. L., and B. Poon, eds. 1999. "Reflections of First-Year Teachers on School Culture: Questions, Hopes, and Challenges." *New Directions for School Leadership* 11. San Francisco: Jossey-Bass.

DuFour, R. 2002. "The Learning Centered Principal." *Educational Leadership* May.

Dussault, M., and S. Thibodeau. 1997. "Professional Isolation and Performance at Work of School Principals." *Journal of School Leadership* 7 (5): 521–36.

Elmore, R. F. 1999. *Leadership of Large-Scale Improvement in American Education.* Washington, DC: Albert Shanker Institute.

———. 2000. *Building a New Structure for School Leadership.* Washington, DC: Albert Shanker Institute.

———. 2001. Electronic transcript of the conference proceedings. Educational Leadership Conference, 17–18 May, Center for Educational Leadership and the CUNY Consortium for Educational Leadership.

———. December 2001. *Time Is Money That Has Been Spent.* Hartford: Connecticut Center for School Change.

———. January 2002. *Leverage Points and Improvement Strategies.* Hartford: Connecticut Center for School Change.

———. February 2002. *Leverage Points and Improvement Strategies: Continued.* Hartford: Connecticut Center for School Change.

Elmore, R. F., with D. Burney. 1997. *Investing in Teacher Learning: Staff Development and Instructional Improvement in Community School District #2, New York City.* New York: National Commission on Teaching and America's Future and Consortium for Policy Research in Education.

Fine, M. 1989. "Silencing and Nurturing Voice in an Improbable Context: Urban Adolescents in Public School." In *Clinical Pedagogy: The State and Cultural Struggle,* eds. H. Giroux and P. McLaren. New York: State University of New York Press.

Fink, E., and L. B. Resnick. 2001. "Developing Principals as Instructional Leaders." *Phi Delta Kappan* 82 (8): 598–606.

Fisher, R., and A. Sharp, with J. Richardson. 1998. *Getting It Done: From to Lead When You're Not in Charge.* New York: Harper Business.

Fisher, R., and W. Ury, with B. Patton. 1991. *Getting to Yes: Negotiating Agreement Without Giving In.* New York: Penguin Books.

Foundation Center, The. 2001. *The Foundation Center's Guide to Proposal Writing.* 3d. ed. New York: The Foundation Center.

Fullan, M. 1993. *Change Forces: Probing the Depths of Educational Reform.* London: Routledge Falmer.

———. 1997. *What's Worth Fighting for in the Principalship?* New York: Teachers College Press.

———. 1999. *Change Forces: The Sequel.* Philadelphia: Falmer Press.

———. 2001. *Leading in a Culture of Change.* San Francisco, CA: Jossey-Bass.

Fullan, M., and A. Hargreaves. 1996. *What's Worth Fighting for in Your School?* New York: Teachers College Press.

Fullan, M., and C. Rolheiser, 2001. "Dealing with Resistance." Presentation at Breaking Through Change Barriers Conference, May.

Gewirtzman, L., and E. Fink. n.d. "Realignment of Policies and Resources." New York: Cross City Campaign for Urban School Reform.

Glasman, N. S., and L. D. Glasman. 1997. "Connecting the Preparation of School Leaders to the Practice of School Leadership." *Peabody Journal of Education* 72 (2): 3–20.

Goleman, D. 1998. *Working with Emotional Intelligence.* New York: Bantam Doubleday Dell.

Griffiths, D. E. 1988. *Educational Administration: Reform PDQ or RIP.* University Council for Educational Administration, Occasional Paper No. 8312. Tempe, AZ: Arizona State University.

Griffiths, D. E., R. T. Stout, and P. B. Forsyth. 1988. *Leaders for America's Schools.* Berkeley, CA: McCutchan.

Hargrove, R. 1998. *Mastering the Art of Creative Collaboration.* New York: McGraw-Hill.

Healey, F., and J. De Stefano. 1997. *Education Reform Support: A Framework for Scaling Up School Reform.* Washington, DC: Abel 2 Clearinghouse for Basic Education.

Heifetz, R. A., and M. Linsky. 2002. *Leadership on the Line: Staying Alive Through the Dangers of Leading.* Cambridge, MA: Harvard Business School Press.

Hertling, E. 1999. *Conducting a Principal Search.* ERIC Document Reproduction Service No. ED 436815.

Isaacs, W. 1999. *Dialogue and the Art of Thinking Together: A Pioneering Approach to Communicating in Business and in Life.* New York: Currency.

Jacobs, H. 1997. *Mapping the Big Picture.* Alexandra, VA: ASCD.

Katzenbach, J. R., and D. K. Smith. 1993. *The Wisdom of Teams: Creating the High-Performance Organization.* New York: Harper Business.

Keller, B. 1998. "Principals' Shoes Are Hard to Fill, Study Finds." *Education Week* 17 (27). Online and available at: www.edweek.org/ew/ew_printstory.cfm?slug=27prin.h17.

Kempner, K. 1991. "Getting into the Castle of Educational Administration." *Peabody Journal of Education* 66 (3): 104–23.

Kim, D. H. 1994. *Systems Archetypes I: Diagnosing Systemic Issues and Designing High-Leverage Interventions.* Toolbox Reprint Series. Waltham, MA: Pegasus Communications.

Kirkland, K., and S. Manoogian. 1998. *Ongoing Feedback: How to Get It, How to Use It.* Greensboro, NC: Center for Creative Leadership Press.

Knowles, M. S. 1980. *The Modern Practice of Adult Education: From Pedagogy to Andragogy.* Englewood Cliffs, NJ: Cambridge Adult Education, Prentice Hall Regents.

Kohl, H. R. 1994. *"I Won't Learn From You": And Other Thoughts on Creative Maladjustment.* New York: New Press.

Krogh, G. von, K. Ichijo, and I. Nonaka. 2000. *Enabling Knowledge Creation: How to Unlock the Mystery of Tacit Knowledge and Release the Power of Innovation.* New York: Oxford University Press.

Lewis, A. 1998. "Teachers in the Driver's Seat." *The Harvard Educational Letter* 14 (2): 1–4.

Lieberman, A., and M. W. McLaughlin. 1992. "Networks for Educational Change: Powerful and Problematic." *Phi Delta Kappan* 73 (9): 673 77.

Madfes, T. J., and J. H. Shulman, eds. 2000. *Dilemmas in Professional Development: A Case-Based Approach to Improving Practice.* San Francisco: West Ed.

McGrath, D. and P. Kuriloff. November 1999. "They're Going to Tear the Doors Off This Place: Upper Middle Class Parent School Involvement and the Educational Opportunities of Other People's Children." *Education Policy* 13 (5).

McLaughlin, M. W., and J. E. Talbert. 1993. *Contexts That Matter for Teaching and Learning: Strategic Opportunities for Meeting the Nation's Educational Goals.* Stanford, CA: Stanford University, Center for Research on the Context of Secondary School Teaching.

McTighe, J. and G. Wiggins. 1999. *The Understanding by Design Handbook.* Alexandra, VA: ASCD.

Mehan, H. 1996. "Beneath the Skin and Between the Ears: A Case Study in the Politics of Representation." In *Understanding Practice*, eds. S. Chaiklin and J. Love, pp. 241–268. Cambridge: Cambridge University Press.

Merz, C., and G. Furman. 1997. *Community and Schools: Promise and Paradox.* New York: Teachers College Press.

Mindell, A. 1995. *Sitting in the Fire: Large Group Transformation Using Conflict and Diversity.* Portland, OR: Lao Tse Press.

Morey, D., M. Maybury, and B. Thuraisingham, eds. 2000. *Knowledge Management: Classic and Contemporary Works.* Cambridge, MA: MIT Press.

National Commission on Teaching and America's Future. 1996. *What Matters Most: Teaching for America's Future.* New York: National Commission on Teaching and America's Future.

Natriello, G. 1999. "Time and the Review Process." *Teachers College Record* 100 (4): 697–701. Online and available at: www.tcrecord.org/Content.asp?ContentID=1035.

Nonaka, I., and H. Takeuchi. 1995. *The Knowledge-Creating Company: How Japanese Companies Create the Dynamics of Innovation.* New York: Oxford University Press.

Orozco, L. 1994. "Building Arks: Collaboration for School Administrators." *Journal of CAPEA* 6: 9–18.

———. 2001. "Saving the New Endangered Species: The Role of Higher Education in the Preparation and Success of School Leaders." *Educational Leadership and Administration* 13: 3–8.

Patton, M. 1996. *Utilization-Focused Evaluation: The New Century Text.* Thousand Oaks, CA: Sage Publications.

Pelika, S. L. 2000. Shaping the Work Environment for Teachers: How Principals Can Learn to Support Instructional Reform. Paper presented at the annual meeting of the American Educational Research Association, 24–28 April, New Orleans, Louisiana. ERIC Document Reproduction Service No. ED 454623.

Piaget, J. 1929. *The Child's Conception of the World.* New York: Harcourt, Brace Jovanovich.

Pinson, L., and J. Jinnett. 1996. *Anatomy of a Business Plan: A Step-by-Step Guide to Starting Smart, Building the Business, and Securing Your Company's Future.* 3d ed. Chicago: Upstart.

Pollack, M. 2001. "How the Question We Ask Most About Race in Education Is the Question We Most Suppress." *Educational Researcher* 30 (9): 2–12.

Pugach, M. C., and L. J. Johnson. 2002. *Collaborative Practitioners, Collaborative Schools.* 2d ed. Denver, CO: Love Publishing.

Ravitch, D. 1988. *The Great School Wars: A History of the New York City Public Schools.* New York: Basic Books.

Resnick, L. B., and M. W. Hall. 1998. "Learning Organizations for Sustainable Education Reform." *Daedalus* 127 (4): 89–118.

Resnick, L. B., and S. Nelson-Le Gall. 1997. "Socializing Intelligence." In *Piaget, Vygotsky and Beyond*, eds. L. Smith, J. Dockrell, and P. Tomlinson, pp. 145–58. London: Routledge.

Sanders, W. L., and S. P. Horn. 1994. "The Tennessee Value-Added Assessment System (TVAAS): Mixed-Model Methodology in Educational Assessment." *Journal of Personnel Evaluation in Education* 8: 299–311.

Sanders, W. L., A. M. Saxton, and S. P. Horn. 1998. "The Tennessee Value-Added Assessment System (TVAAS): A Quantitative, Outcomes-Based Approach to Educational Assessment." In *Grading Teacher, Grading Schools: Is Student Achievement a Valid Evaluation Measure?*, ed. J. Milliman. Thousand Oaks, CA: Corwin Press.

Sapon-Shevin, M. 1994. *Playing Favorites: Gifted Education and the Disruption of Community.* Albany: SUNY Press.

Schön, D. A. 1983. *The Reflective Practitioner: How Professionals Think in Action.* New York: Basic Books.

————. 1987. *Educating the Reflective Practitioner: Toward a New Design for Teaching and Learning in the Professions.* San Francisco: Jossey-Bass.

Senge, P. 1990. "The Leader's New Work: Building Learning Organizations." *Sloan Management Review* 32 (1).

Senge, P., A. Kleiner, C. Roberts, R. B. Ross, and B. J. Smith. 1994. *The Fifth Discipline Fieldbook: Strategies and Tools for Building a Learning Organization.* New York: Doubleday.

Senge, P., A. Kleiner, C. Roberts, G. Roth, R. Ross, and B. Smith. 1999. *The Dance of Change: The Challenges of Sustaining Momentum in Learning Organizations.* New York: Doubleday.

Senge, P., N. Cambron-McCabe, T. Lucas, B. Smith, J. Dutton, and A. Kleiner. 2000. *Schools That Learn: A Fifth Discipline Fieldbook for Educators, Parents, and Everyone Who Cares About Education.* New York: Doubleday.

Spillane, J., R. Halverson, and J. B. Diamond. 2001. "Investigating School Leadership Practice: A Distributive Perspective." *Educational Researcher* 30 (3).

Stacey, R. D. 1996. *Complexity and Creativity in Organizations.* San Francisco: Berrett-Koehler.

Stein, S., and H. Book. 2000. *The EQ Edge.* Toronto, Canada: Stoddart Publishing.

Steinberg, J. 2000. "Nation's Schools Struggling to Find Enough Principals." *New York Times,* 3 September, A1.

Sterman, J. D. 2000. *Business Dynamics: Systems Thinking and Modeling for a Complex World.* Boston: Irwin McGraw-Hill.

Stewart, T. A. 2001. *The Wealth of Knowledge: Intellectual Capital and the Twenty-First Organization.* New York: Currency.

Stone, D., B. Patton, and S. Heen. 1999. *Difficult Conversations: How to Discuss What Matters Most.* New York: Viking.

Thurston, P., R. Clift, and M. Schacht. 1993. "Preparing Leaders for Change-Oriented Schools." *Phi Delta Kappan* 75: 259–65.

Tichy, N. M., with E. B. Cohen. 1997. *Leadership Engine: How Winning Companies Build Leaders at Every Level.* New York: HarperCollins.

Tucker, M. S., and J. B. Codding, eds. 2002. *The Principal Challenge: Leading and Managing Schools in an Era of Accountability.* San Francisco: Jossey-Bass.

Van Meter, E., and J. Murphy. 1997. *Using ISLLC Standards to Strengthen Preparation Programs in School Administration.* Washington, DC: Council of Chief State School Officers.

Wenglinsky, H. 2000. "How Teaching Matters." Report by the Educational Testing Service.

Wilmore, E. L., and J. J. McNeil Jr. 1999. "Who Will Lead Our Schools?" *International Journal of Educational Reform* 8 (4): 365–73.

Yankelovich, D. 1999. *The Magic of Dialogue: Transforming Conflict into Cooperation.* New York: Simon & Schuster.

INDEX